Fair Dinkum Mates Tales

Geoff Cobden

Copyright © Geoff Cobden 2017

First Published in 2017 by
Level Heading

All rights reserved. Without limiting the rights under copyright reserved above, no part of this publication may be reproduced, stored in or introduced into a retrieval system, or transmitted, in any form or by any means (electronic, mechanical, photocopying, recording or otherwise), without the prior written permission of the copyright owner.

ISBN 978-0-6481726-0-4

Line drawings by the author.
Picture on page 83 from Pixabay under the
Creative Commons License COO and require no attribution.
Picture page 101 Public Domain original source fremantleports.com.au
Picture page 161 by Donaldytong, licensed under COO.

A catalogue record for this book is available from the National Library of Australia

On notification, any inadvertent copyright omissions
will be corrected in a future edition.

Design and layout by Level Heading – levelheading.com

Level Heading

Contents

Foreword	5
Time	7
Spinner's Reward	8
Last Reflection	10
Lenny	12
Bradman	16
The Preacher	17
Shaggy Ridge	22
Home	25
The Swamp	26
The Punt Gun	28
Cop That	32
Guests	34
Breached	40
Salad	43
Crappy Shot	45
One Shot	48
Chicklings	50
Punt Limbo	51
Poor Lenny	55
Life Savers	57
Spinner's Reward	58
The Frog	61
The Insides of Old Perc	66
The Garden Postal Chute	70
Trapper Jack	73
Business Partners	78
Spotting Rats	81
Look Up to Your Peeers	84
Underground Adventures	87
The Snack	90
Double Trouble	96
Maritime Cover-up	101
Gotcha	104
Wrecked 'em	107
Lost and Found	111
The Long Drop	118
Thing a Thong of Thickness	123
Summer Love	126
Blind Mullet	130
A Bloody Day	133
Rani	140
Big Colin	147
Jonesy	151
The Pussycat Incident	153
The Warren	158
Acknowledgments	162

Foreword

"Fair Dinkum Mates Tales" came about because of the reminiscing of family and friends. You know what it's like, relating events of the past to engrossed listeners, young and old who suggest, "You could write a book about all these stories." So here it is. All the stories in this reflective narration are true (even the ones that aren't), although some names have been altered to protect the guilty. Some have been left in to create embarrassment.

As I'm approaching an age where old mates and relatives are dropping like flies, I thought, "why not pass on some of these anecdotes and short stories to amuse and enlighten those that follow of how things happened in and around the Baby Boomer years ... Before it's too late."

I hope you enjoy this variety of stories as much as I did remembering them.

Geoff Cobden.

To those who don't understand the phrase "Fair Dinkum", it is best described as:
>Truthful, Honest, Real, True Dinks, Honest to God, Unadulterated, Sincere, No Bulldust, True, The Gospel.

Time

It flashed, it's gone, it disappeared,
It came, it went, like wasted years,
Where have they gone? Those memories past,
I blinked, the hours slipped so fast.

They turned to months, the faces fade,
The crown of silk has slowly greyed,
They then transform the years of thought,
Of distant loves and dreams cut short.

Those goals desired but not achieved,
Of webs that Father Time has weaved,
And how our journey's many trails,
Direct us to our Holy grail.

What is it that we've so misplaced?
That left us with such speed and haste,
It has no rhythm or no rhyme,
What's gone? It's obvious, it's time.

Spinner's Reward

He'd learnt to fish when but a youth,
And loved it with a lust,
He'd fished for fun, and just for sport,
And once to earn a crust.

It wasn't that the man was tight.
Or keen to save a quid,
It's just he hated waste,
And losing spinners blew his lid.

He'd strolled a hundred streams,
From the Murray to the Yarra,
Catching Rainbows, Cod and Yellas
By the bagful, and the Barra.

The thought of losing spinners,
Was to him like spilling wine,
He'd strip off to his birthday suit,
And follow down the line.

One afternoon in April,
With the river running fast,
He got caught a proper beauty,
And he'd only had one cast.

So with certain parts quite frozen,
And a face resembling blue,
He undertook the rescue,
With a vengeance seen by few.

The line ran round an old gum branch,
And through a patch of weed,
And snagged upon the object,
That had done the dirty deed.

The spinner wouldn't shift,
But the object might with force,
So he heaved with all his might,
and nature took its course.

Struggling to the surface,
Gasping air and feeling sick,
His eyes befell the culprit,
And his tongue began to lick.

In his arms he clutched a roll of wire,
Barbed and rusty brown,
And a hundred glistening spinners,
Like a coronation crown.

They dangled there in clusters,
A dozen at a time,
The accumulated losses,
Plus a mile of tangled line.

It took a morning's work,
To remove the lures attached,
A labour most rewarding, though
His hands and arms were scratched.

So pleased was he with all his luck,
He gave his thigh a whack,
And feeling not the slightest guilt,
He threw the object back.

Last Reflection

Rusted cans and white clay pipes,
Bottles glistening in the early light,
Decayed remains of the old oil lamp,
That lit the camp in the dead calm night.

There's a bent horseshoe near a stump cut clean,
The boiler dormant that once made steam,
Sun-dried bricks where the scrub now grows,
Breakaway slopes contoured dry blows.

A whisk of breeze stirs long dead embers,
The same warm breeze the old man remembers,
Seventy years had come and past,
When as a lad he felt the blast.

He reminisced of the green rock moss,
Of starry nights and the Southern Cross,
Of the old horse Nel, dusty and brown,
And the heartbreak endured when she was put down.

There by the creek ever dry, full of sand,
Sandalwood trees, and a Salmon gum stand,
Were the blows that he'd worked as a lad twelve years old,
And there by the creek he'd found his first gold.

Tears welled deep in tired old eyes,
As he thought of the crows and the dingo cries,
The flapping of canvas, the scrape of the shovel,
The piling of quartz, separation of rubble.

The thump of the stamp, and call of the mail,
Bore water clear and lapping the pail,
Aroma of damper and grinding of grain,
Fragrance of flowers and sweet smell of rain.

Yes, to others this ruin would seem just a mine,
But old men who dream regard it a shrine,
Each relic of interest, each rusty old can,
That litters the landscape, has a story, a plan.

He gazed one more time at the memories of youth,
Excused his return with reflections of truth,
As the breeze rustled leaves he thought of his bride,
And lay by the creek and peacefully died.

Lenny

Lenny Ross was quite a man, a ball of Australian muscle, six feet two in the old scale and not an ounce of fat. Being brought up on the farm had a lot of bearing on his stature, which was tall and athletic, what with all the chores that came with the job. His skin was taut and tanned, his hair dark, from a distance close enough to black. The eyes were dark brown and ever so slightly squinted, a natural reaction developed from all the outdoors activities in the hot sun. His chin was squarish with a central cleft that gave him that film star, "Gone with the Wind" look. The local girls loved him, and he took full advantage of their admiration. Until the Lister diesel milking machine was installed in 1936, the herd was milked by hand. This meant he shared a rolling roster with his dad John, and brothers George and Stan. That was his early duty, if it wasn't his turn to milk he got to sleep in an extra couple of hours, where, after breakfast an hour of log splitting was required as, even in summer, the wood heater had to be kept alight.

Then there was fencing, miles of it. Dad had purchased his first tractor, a 1939 Ford Ferguson N9. It was the first to come with a three-point linkage and electric start, and the posthole digger attachment was a godsend. It saved so much back-breaking work, but the posts still had to be lumped around … they didn't set themselves. They were cut and split in a forest some ten miles to the north-west from home, no decent fencing trees remained in the surrounding areas, only stunted firewood material, the few that were good enough, were preserved for stock shelter and, as Dad called it, "aesthetic beauty". They were transported back to the property on the back of Dad's secondhand 1934 flatbed 1.5 ton

Chevrolet. It saved half a day's travel, went where you pointed it, didn't have to be groomed or fed, and didn't fart in your face. Sal was renowned for that. Sal was a gentle giant, a beautiful camel-coloured Clydesdale with a gorgeous silvery mane and long silver anklets.

She was eighteen hands high and was a great mate. She knew where to turn while using implements without so much as a whistle or a click of the tongue, and didn't have a nasty bone in her body. But she did present another set of tasks in feeding, grooming, shoeing and housing, which all took time and effort. She became pretty much obsolete when the tractor arrived, the amount of ground the machine could cover in a day with all the various attachments that were available was amazing. So Sal spent the rest of her days in peaceful retirement in the bottom paddock with her best mate, a young steer that had lost both its eyes to the dreaded "pink eye", a severe case of conjunctivitis. They'd graze together all day, and of an evening, settle down together nuzzling.

"OPENING THE BAYS"

They enjoyed each other's company for many years.

After the crops were sown, the irrigation bays had to be watered and patrolled day and night. This entailed trudging the entire sown area with a shovel over one shoulder, a hurricane lantern and a stout pair of gumboots. As each bay was filled it was closed off with the shovel, moving on to the next unopened bay. The feeder channel was breached about two shovel widths letting in the precious life-giving water to gurgle and swirl into the paddock.

As it slowly crept down the bay, a host of grasshoppers, crickets, and all kinds of creepy-crawlies would move ahead of the wall of water. This in turn invited water birds of all kinds to fly in and feast on the smorgasbord of goodies, which they devoured with glee, along with truckloads of newly sown grain. George, Len's elder brother, always said that the birds could smell the fresh water from many miles away, and could distinguish between permanent and newly covered ground.

Some bays, during really good seasons, would have to be resown two or even three times because of duck infestation, at great expense to the farmer.

The operator could handle around four bays at a time, as it took half a night to fill each one, it meant that those on duty had to be on call at all hours. If a bay overfilled, the containing banks may be breeched, which not only wasted precious, costly water, it could flood an unprepared paddock. It could also make a muddy mess of the bank that couldn't be repaired until it dried out. On reaching the bay in question, if it was discovered that it wasn't quite full, then a quiet sit under the stars on the bank was in order. Len remembered these times as exceptionally pleasant experiences. It was a wondrous thing, he thought, to lie on the bank cradling his head in his cupped hands, staring at the stars on a clear summer's evening. The breeze caressing his face as it cooled down over the new water, not a sole for miles, the soft gurgle of flowing water, crickets chirping, distant calling of teal and black duck carried on the night air, and the starlit sky above always provided a lightshow of shooting stars and meteors streaking across the sky, like silent chalk on a blackboard.

It really put a bloke in his place, he thought.

Bradman

Len's father John had once recalled during the Great Rabbit Plague years earlier, while trudging out to the water with shovel and lantern, how he had stopped to light his pipe. This required two hands so the lantern and shovel were placed on the ground. Out of the darkness a rabbit appeared, running straight for the light, then another and another. Dad picked up the shovel and using the lantern as a wicket, became the Bradman of the bush, rabbits being slogged to all points of the compass for four.

On another occasion, while sitting on the channel bank waiting for a bay to fill, he sensed a movement to his left. There, on the bank not two feet away was a large tiger snake with a frog hanging from his mouth. One of Australia's most deadly snakes was beside him hunting dinner.

The Preacher

Dad was quite a card and renowned for his quick wit and humour. During the early thirties, old John (old was hardly the word, John was killed by a falling tree branch at only 54 years of age) received a visit from the local preacher Mr Harrison. Mr Harrison didn't get to meet his more remote prospective parishioners so he would hitch up the horse and buggy and spend two days a week travelling around the Shire, introducing himself to all he could meet with a view to encouraging them to return the effort and venture into Kerang for a Sunday morning service. There was Dad on top of a low rise, when the preacher trotted up in a cloud of dust. He alighted from the buggy, introduced himself and proceeded to butter John up with some heartening words.

"My," he said, doing a complete circle with outstretched arms, surveying the expanse of paddocks and greenery the vista presented, "you and the Lord have certainly done wonders with this property, haven't you?"

Dad removed his sweat-stained hat, wiped a bead of perspiration from his brow and replied thoughtfully, "you should have seen it when he had it."

He never did get Dad to attend a service but enjoyed his company enough to visit once a month, usually turning up with a fruitcake that Mrs Harrison had baked the day before, and he never went home empty handed. Dad always reciprocated with tomatoes, or cantaloupe or a dozen other goodies from his extensive vegetable garden. He did get the last word, as he presided over John's funeral after the tragic accident.

After the crops had grown they were harvested. Mowing, raking bailing and stacking was hot, hard work, always carried out in the summer period after spring growth; and Len hated it.

His eyes and nose would run with incurable hay-fever, and every prickly itchy seed and burr found their way into all his creases and folds of skin, and clung to his sweaty clothing like "shit to a blanket", Len cursed. Red welts appeared and itched worse than the bites of mosquitoes from the nearby swamp. The only action that gave relief was to wade into the channel or dam fully clothed and dunk himself like a teabag. What relief it provided.

The top eighteen inches or so of water, warmed by the sun, was akin to the best saunas of Europe but beneath that layer it was absolutely freezing, it refreshed and revived the senses enough for another hour or two of toil.

Before the tractor, all of the crops were stooked. A timely process that saw the sheaves cut by a reaper-binder and formed by hand into small pyramids (stooks). But with the modern bailer hauled along behind the tractor the process became a whole lot easier. Some claimed that the earlier method was still better as no dust found its way into the feed. If fed to expensive horses or

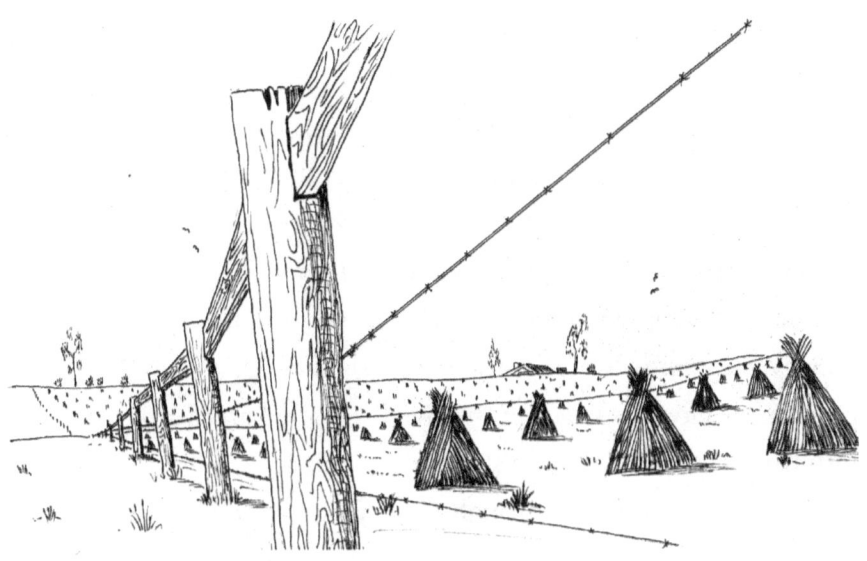

livestock, internal bleeding could occur if dust was consumed, a definite no-no for racehorses.

Luckily, with Dad and the brothers to share the load, each got to practise their leisure pursuits.

Len played cricket, being a top fast bowler for the local Appin side, and loved hunting and fishing. He couldn't wait to shower after a hot day's toil, grab the shotgun, a beautiful single barrelled Greener, and a handful of cartridges, and trudge four miles to the Loddon River. On the way he'd stalk along the low sides of channel banks and dams, popping his head up slowly at various intervals with intention of ambushing ducks or other game that might be unlucky enough to be in his sights.

Any game that was bagged was hidden in a boxthorn or at the base of a fencepost until his return. You couldn't trust foxes or hawks spotting it before he could make it back, it'd be gone in no time.

Reaching the Loddon was like stepping into another time zone. The river and surrounding habitat was untouched by man and in the same state that the famous explorers Burke and Wills must have found it in 1860. There was, and probably still is, an old dead tree beside the river with the words C13 carved on the east face, facing the river. This they reckoned depicted camp thirteen, of either the original expedition or one of the search parties. Fences stopped well short of the river, some 200 yards in places, to allow for the regular seasonal flood peaks. The terrain became salt bush, long grasses, and stunted trees on the plains with accumulated growth the closer one got to the river, the open areas graduating into thicker bushes and tall shady river gums.

The river meandered through natural undulating rises, with bends so acute that sections looped back on themselves, so you could walk the entire loop to find yourself only fifty yards from the starting point. Great spots for ambushing wild ducks, and the adjacent flood plains were full of rabbits, foxes and wild boars. At a number of these quiet shady bends, mounds of shells, thousands of them, were evidence of earlier inhabitants. What an idyllic, peaceful home it must have been, albeit seasonal. Plenty of water, game, and fish (though none of the introduced species we mentioned earlier), kangaroo, wallaby, duck and shellfish as well as native cod, yellow belly, and bream (grunter), firewood in abundance and shelter from the elements.

On one occasion, George had discovered a human skull beside one of the mounds and, before burying it, solemnly declared that it was the skull of a woman. "How the bloody hell do you know that?" Len enquired unbelieving of George's newly acquired archaeological knowledge. "It has to be," he replied, "Its mouth is open."

The river water was pristine and clear in those pre-European carp days. Len loved to fish and the native fish were abundant.

Even the introduced English perch (redfin) were present then, and it was nothing to cast a lure into the clear waters and witness half a dozen fish fighting one another to get at it. All this experience, the hard work on the farm, miles and miles of walking the channel banks, irrigation and hikes to the river, not to mention carrying his catch, be it a brace of rabbits, half a dozen ducks or a bag of fish were to stand him in good stead when, in 1942, he was called up for military service.

"BENDS SO ACUTE THAT SECTIONS LOOPED BACK ON THEMSELVES."

Shaggy Ridge

After a crash course training, Len served in New Guinea in the 2/16 battalion 21st brigade and experienced all the hardships of Shaggy Ridge and jungle warfare. He couldn't believe it, after being brought up in the Kerang area, the highest bit of ground being Pyramid Hill, which represented a mere pimple on the landscape compared to the Ramu Valley and the Finisterre Range. Shaggy Ridge was a six and a half kilometre long razorbacked ridge that was a virtual ladder climb of hell. Shaggy Ridge was the site of the main Japanese defensive that blocked access to the Ramu Valley and its connecting access roads to the north coast. It was vital to the war effort to win this ground and connect with Australian forces advancing from the east. No matter how fit you were, nothing, no preparation whatsoever could prepare a soldier for the mud, the murderous inclines, lack of proper sustenance, mosquitoes and a dozen exotic illnesses, but Len's early upbringing made him a little more prepared than the poor buggers that had

been enrolled from the big smoke. They did it really tough but never complained. He was unable to hide his admiration for the courage and determination these blokes exhibited.

Lenny experienced the initial attack on Shaggy Ridge, the morning of 27 December 1943. Hunkered down in a hand dug foxhole he waited with the rest of B Company on the razorback while three and a half thousand twenty-five pound bombs rained down on Shaggy Ridge. Every Japanese vantage point was strafed and bombed by Australian Boomerangs and American Kitty Hawks. The crescendo of sound was unbelievable. Shock waves pounded down the ridge and rubble rained on the troops like a Vesuvius eruption. Then at the precise command at nine a.m. the attack began. They scrambled out of their protective trenches and clambered up the precipitous slopes, with Australian artillery still raining down, bullets whizzing past, and the enemy close enough to hurl grenades.

A grenade bounced off Len's shoulder before exploding harmlessly below the ridge. A bullet ripped through his uniform under the armpit and dropped the poor bugger behind him. Still they pushed on through the smoke and flying rubble, the hail of lead and the screaming of Japanese wounded. Funny, Len thought, they don't take pain as well as our boys. He also noted that when your life's on the line all your senses sharpen in intensity, his peripheral vision was on maximum alert, and his reflexes were instant. There was movement above and to the left, it was as if in slow motion. The Jap saw him at the same moment. Len didn't even aim, it was like an extension of his arm. The Bren gun stuttered and a face disappeared. He didn't think he even heard the Bren. The attack didn't last all that long and they captured the feature known as "the pimple" and another 100 yards or so of the ridge. B Company's mission had been successful and was then relieved by D Company which captured the next two knolls on the ridge the next day. The Japanese counter-attacked and fought hand-to-hand for many days, bombarding the Australians constantly with Mountain Guns. The action continued north and south along the entire spine which was Shaggy Ridge, until the 1st of February 1944 where, after attack and counter-attack, continuous bombardments, hand-to-hand fighting and finally the last hill, known as Crater Hill, was pounded with bombs and artillery for days to soften up the enemy in preparation of a final assault.

When companies from each of the 2/9th and 2/10th advanced up the hill they discovered it blown to kingdom come, and not an enemy in sight.

The capture of Shaggy Ridge cost Australia 46 killed and 147 wounded. The Japanese had over 500 casualties inflicted on them with 244 confirmed dead. Meanwhile, earlier that month, after the initial assault on Shaggy ridge, Len and the 2/16th had been returned to Port Moresby, mopping up for two months and returned to Australia on March 20th.

On 3rd June, they were shipped to Borneo, at Balikpapan, where extremely heavy fighting was encountered. Another bullet had creased Len's person, this time his Slouch Hat, which sported an entry hole at the front right and exited centre top … he couldn't for the life of him understand why he was still alive. It must have entered at a point which allowed it to angle upwards and exit above his left ear. He participated in patrols until the war ended on August 15th, then formed part of the occupational forces in the Celebes until late January 1946. At last it was over, he sailed for home on 2nd of February having felt full well, he'd done his bit.

Home

On his return in '46, the farm was just as he had remembered it, so isolated and detached from the big bad world he had just participated in. His brother George was now running the place on his own, as Stan had moved out and married. George had lost an eye midway through the War when chipping at a bolt under the tractor, but had acclimatized himself to the disability. He could still shoot as good as Len, maybe better. He once remarked to Len that, "you are one of the best shots I've ever seen, and you know damn well I can beat you." They displayed a typical brotherly rivalry in everything. Hunting and fishing, Len played cricket, George was a top footballer, and both enjoyed a fiery game of six-handed euchre with visiting hunters.

The Swamp

The property was located on the eastern shoreline of a large swamp. The milking shed having a commanding view over an expanse of water that was peppered with dead trees and stumps. To the southern shoreline, some intermittent stands of cumbungi (a species of reed), and to the north, the main body of water narrowed to a small isthmus, then opened up again to a large body comprising nearly all cumbungi interconnected with winding channels and islands ... a great spot for decoys and "great blackie country," George would say, in reference to the hunter's prime target, the Pacific black duck, or blackie. This was the largest of the target species, there was one larger, the Mountain Duck, but despite it being listed as legal game, hunters of experience didn't bother with it, as it was hard to pluck and tough as old boots.

The area attracted ducks and other water birds by the tens of thousands. Their numbers included, grey and chestnut teal, black

duck, pink ear, hardhead, blue wing shovelers, wood duck, and mountain duck. Rarer species like the bluebill and musk ducks were regular inhabitants and the even rarer freckled duck dropped in at times. Coots, water hens, swans and pelicans were permanent residents, and seasonal visits from snipe would stop by from their migratory journey from Russia, and on some very wet years the swamp was graced with the presence of brolgas and whistling and plumed tree ducks from up north. The place was a wonderland for waterfowl, and as a result, attracted hunters and wildfowlers from all over the state.

George told of his father's recollection that, "they were so thick you couldn't get your fingers between them."

The Punt Gun

He told of an earlier time when the local traders had operated a punt gun. This consisted of a large flat-bottomed boat or raft, camouflaged with eucalyptus branches and bales of straw. The gun, which could fire over a pound of shot up to no. 4 size, had a muzzle width of over two inches (50mm) and was over twelve feet (3.6m) in length. It was lashed tight on both sides of the punt and secured on a bed of straw bales, which were covered with hessian bags. These prevented loose straw from fowling the mechanism. Accompanying the Punt Gun were the beaters, all in small flat-bottomed craft, also camouflaged and stealthy. Their job was to line up on either side of the Punt Gun across the swamp, with the operator lying down flat in the punt, both arms paddling under the water out of view so as not to spook the birds. Together they slowly advanced, quietly herding and pushing hundreds of ducks towards the shoreline. It may have been flock mentality, but it seemed that all birds other than ducks slipped to

"PUNT GUN"

one side and quietly paddled away, whereas the ducks preferred to pack together tightly until the last moment. Stragglers at the sides, sensing danger would lift and curl away to safety behind the flotilla, but the main flock must have felt safety in numbers until it was too late.

The entire manoeuvre could take half a day's stealthy paddling, gently pushing, slowly closing in on the mob. The slightest mistake jeopardised the whole hunt.

Complete quiet and stealth, stalking the quarry, no standing up, no talking, no splashing. As they were always downwind of the mob the odd puff of a pipe was allowed, but toilet breaks had to be accomplished lying down. When the numbers were tight enough, the Punt Gun was slowly jockeyed into position. After a predetermined stump, tree or some such other marker was reached, usually at a distance that would allow the Punt Gun to attain its utmost effect (around 50–60 yards), the accompanying line of beaters would quietly glide to a halt. The gunner prepared the shot, and at his signals a chorus of whistles rang out from the line. This encouraged hundreds of ducks to raise their heads in unison, craning their necks to see what the commotion was all about. The punt gunner's assistant would then fire a 12-gauge round into the flock, and a split second later as a thousand ducks rose from the water the shot was taken, and over one pound of lead pellets raked through the mob as they were at their most vulnerable, lifting from the water, decimating all before its deadly hail. The beaters on either side then came into action with 12-gauge guns picking off the survivors of the main onslaught. It was not uncommon to see over 100 ducks taken using this method, the recoil sending the Punt craft in reverse up to half a cricket pitch. The rest of the day would see the birds sorted,

cleaned, plucked, singed, washed and prepared for market, then divided up among all the participants.

The punt gun was banned in Australia many years ago, but is still employed by water fowlers in Britain, but a much smaller gauge.

George (above) was also a large man, just as tall as Len but a lot thicker set, about 18 stone (250 kg) and about 10 years older. He was a lovely, quietly spoken man with an amiable smile and a great sense of humour. Self-motivated, he ran the farm alone, as the others had married and moved on. George knew nothing else. His loss of an eye refused him any chance of joining the forces, so staying on the land would at least see him contribute to the war effort with grain, milk and meat.

But on top of that he couldn't get a mile past the front gate without feeling homesick.

As long as he was within eyeshot of the tall eucalypt that overshadowed the house he was safe. It was the tallest tree in the district and could be seen for some miles. He slept in the western bedroom comprising a wire-based double bed with wrought iron frame topped off with shiny brass fittings. His ample girth had extended the wire base over the years and it had stretched to the shape of a hammock, but he loved it. The room was encircled by wallboard from the floor up to the window sills where cobweb covered fly-wire finished the walls off.

It received all the afternoon sun which was great in winter, but in summer was a sauna. Be it summer or winter, any guest that was lucky enough to be invited to use the back room, when tiptoeing to the toilet, which was located in the laundry directly opposite George's room, could espy him, on his back in bed, one sheet in summer, one blanket in winter, huge bare feet sticking out the end of the bed, snoring the sleep of an honest farmer. Beside the bed, on a small timber cabinet, perched an alarm clock, a saucer with a spent pipe, and a glass of water, in which were his false teeth and his glass eye. He'd remark that, "I'm keeping an eye on my teeth."

Cop That

During the war, George was sent to Melbourne to be measured up for his glass eye. Travelling down to the big smoke by train was an exciting adventure as he was required to stay on for a few days for fitting and colour matching, he was set up in a double terraced apartment building in South Melbourne. His second floor room, at the top of a set of rickety stairs, was old but adequate. Just a room, an electric jug and an old valve radio beside the bed. But alas, no toilet facilities. If a call of nature eventuated he was expected to make his way downstairs through the rear passage, and navigate, via a rustic garden, to the rear thunder box at the end of the yard. His appointment seen to, he returned through heavy rain to the apartment to while the time away until the next visit was due the next morning.

Here he was, the country boy, all alone, listening to the rain on the corrugated iron bull-nosed balcony roof, admiring the surrounding brick buildings, with a hundred chimneys, disappearing off into the distance. He could see the busy intersection off to the left and occasional pedestrians braving the elements. It may have been the rain on the roof, but George all of a sudden had an overwhelming urge to pee. "Buggered if I'm going out in that rain," he mumbled and approached the wrought iron handrail of the balcony.

"Why not, who's gonna know?" The railing came up to his hips so he was well hidden. He aimed through an opening in the wrought iron and relieved himself with a sigh. Just as he approached the stage of no return, he couldn't stop if he wanted, he heard voices. He peered over the handrail and there, casually walking through his stream of urine, were two of Melbourne's finest constabulary, in full uniform. There's not too many who can lay claim to that, he would boast in future years.

Over the years, George was made known to hundreds of hunters, many of whom would call him to ask of the coming hunting season's prospects. All got to know and love him.

Guests

A small number of these became close personal friends of the Rosses. After many years camping on the edge of the swamp, just outside the farm boundary, a party of hunters, the Cobden brothers, Ken, John and yours truly, Geoff, were invited by George to camp on the higher ground inside the property away from the boggy ground and mosquitoes. He also offered us the use of his milking shed power and access to the water tank. His huge freezer accommodated our bags of game. This arrangement continued for many years until on one exceptionally wet year we were invited to occupy the two rear bedrooms in the house. There we remained for the next 30 years or so. A total of over forty years of friendship and wonderful memories.

The numbers in our party fluctuated up and down as friends and relatives were invited, with George always welcoming and

George at Lake Leagur

hospitable. The opening day's hunt over we would pluck and clean our bag, which on good seasons took us well past noon, and drop them off into the large freezer in George's kitchen. After bogging through the swamp for the best part of half a day, our chores completed, exhaustion set in and the afternoon was spent trying to snooze for a few hours. Not the easiest achievement as the heat and flies could be unbearable. The house accommodation helped that.

As dusk approached, all the hunters would again be at their stations, some wading, others quietly cruising through the shallow waters in low-slung, flat-bottomed punts, usually carrying a load of decoys. A favourite tree or stump was selected. The decoys deployed in the most attractive patterns.

There the operator would alight from his vessel and stand beside it for better manoeuvrability, and safety. If one attempted to shoot on an angle any more acute than 45 degrees from a narrow punt the danger of the recoil upending the craft was maximized. Compared to the early hunt, the evenings were generally quiet affairs. Most birds had moved in large numbers to the safety of channels, dams and refuge sanctuaries located at regular intervals around the state. Occasionally, ducks being disturbed while out feeding or at other waters would drop in and run the gauntlet just on dusk ... if enough hunters ventured out. Usually they were able to land and roost up for the evening undisturbed. But the lack of birds didn't disappoint, just being there was enough.

To witness the orange and scarlet sunsets glowing through a thousand dead trees all reflected on the mirror-like water, like ghostly black figures. There, mud eyes crawled from the murky depths to split their nymph stage casing and emerge to dry their wings in the breeze on the stump beside you and then fly off into the unknown as a new dragonfly.

From Left. Ken, John, Geoff Cobden, Mate Bob Hubbard and George Ross

Musk ducks were splashing the water with head submerged ready to pounce on any morsel that took fright from the splash. The call of coots and water hens, a swan family oblivious to your existence gliding effortlessly past in a slow motion ballet, mum, dad and the kids. Hawks that patrolled together would work in harmony, one spooking a mob of coots which would lift and run at top speed on the water like an aquatic frill neck, while the other selected a straggler and slammed into him at top speed. Pelicans cruised quietly in like a squadron of Lancaster Bombers, and wave after wave of glossy and straw-necked ibis stretched in v-formation, the beat of their wings echoed on the still night air. It was, and still is, an awe inspiring and wondrous sight that captivates the witness, as time became suspended in this orange-tinted wonderland.

After the evening shoot, (or, in most cases, an evening viewing all of the above), everybody would clean up and assemble around the farmhouse kitchen table, where Len, George and the rest of us, including the odd local identity would settle down for a powerful game of six-handed euchre. One of these local identities was a pocket-sized, wiry little shearer named Mick Schmitt. Mick, like the rest of us, loved the evening get-together and delighted in shooting his much larger opponents, (shooting being the euchre terminology for out-trumping an opponent's bid, and being a major factor in their failure to achieve their nominated suit.)

The killing card would be thumped on the table with the force of a karate blow, accompanied by a banzai scream of, "shot you

bastards". Drinks would threaten to topple, coins took to the air. George's pipe, on one occasion, did a neat forward somersault and upended itself on the cat which was dozing at his feet. A whole new meaning came into the term "will someone put the cat out ... " A glass of water did the trick but the cat kept well away from the euchre tournament from that day onwards. "Never, ever, trust a man with his eyes close together," Len would announce in reference to Mick's facial features, and the group would continue the game even harder.

Many jokes, stories, and lies, and a résumé of the day's hunting would fill the room till the early hours. All the world's problems got solved every evening, and they couldn't wait to continue the event the next night.

Eventually, we ended up staying in the house with George. He enjoyed the company, as did we, and for over forty years we enjoyed each other's friendship without so much as one harsh word.

Many times we'd meet his brother Len at the farm. He now resided in Bendigo with his wife Joyce, the love of his life. Together they made regular fishing trips, preferring to camp down at the river, "where I don't have to put up with you blokes perving on me missus," he would offer with mock disgust.

She loved to fish, and Len loved the fact that she also enjoyed one of his favourite pursuits. He would still find his way to the euchre game after dusk most nights, happy to leave Joyce in her quiet, safe camp. No one frequented the river in those days, it was remote and the track in was through a number of gates, after which the camp was reached by no track at all. It was also more than likely that she would have a bag of nice yellowbelly or redfin to boast about on his return. No way was she missing out on potential fun just because he wasn't around. A couple of rods, a warming campfire and a cup of tea kept her in heaven for hours.

Breached

An instance which personified Len's strength and toughness happened during a duck season around 1985. Returning to the farm after a morning fishing down at the Loddon I entered the kitchen to find on the green, bamboo-patterned Laminex table, Len's shotgun, a gaping hole in the breech which was peeled back like a sardine tin.

Beside it, a bloodied handkerchief and an indecipherable note with the only word legible among the bloodied fingerprints, "hospital". I ran out the back door and beckoned hurriedly to George who was coming down the track on the tractor, he alighted and shuffled over to witness my discovery.

We located the number of the Kerang hospital and were informed that, "yes, indeed, Len had presented himself to the emergency department with his forefinger and half his middle finger blown off." Not one for fuss, or hospitals, Len discharged himself in less than a week saying, "I can't stand all the bullshit". He explained the circumstances that led to the accident. It seemed

LENS SHOTGUN. NOTE BREECH PEELED OPEN.

that while waiting under cover at "Dave's Swamp" a small two-hundred-yard-long, but very rewarding irrigation runoff on private land about two miles from the house, he was caught short with a call of nature. Placing his new double barrelled Bentley across his game bag he answered said call. Finished, he washed up in the swamp water and sat back beneath a dead tree to wait for any game that might drop in for a quiet roost. Out of the western sky two shapes appeared sweeping into the north end of the runoff in a long low spiral. As they approached, they banked with wings pointed skywards in preparation to skid to a halt on the wide sheet of water in front of them. He raised the Bentley, swinging from behind; he caught up with the pair, continuing to lead through them a good yard in front, held his line and squeezed. Thump. The concussion nearly deafened him as the right-hand barrel peeled open at the breech, taking his left forefinger and half the middle finger with it. "Funny," he said "there was no pain, just a numbing sensation, probably shock, and ringing ears." The nature break he had taken must have been when the barrels became clogged with mud.

He wrapped them up as best he could, using his handkerchief, collected the remains of his gun, and trudged the two miles back to the farm. Dropping off his gear in the kitchen, he tried to write a note, then drove his Kingswood one handed into the Kerang hospital. With one of George's tea towels wrapped around the wound, he managed to steer the vehicle using the back of his injured hand and crossing his body with his good hand to change gear. We know the rest ... what pain he must have endured, with hardly a complaint ... hardly ... he did complain that his new gun was "buggered" and he missed the "bloody ducks".

The very next day after the accident we located the missing

appendages, or what was left of them, beside the runoff. The meat ants had made a nice mess of them. "Never pick another nose, those buggers," said George, always up for stating the obvious.

DAVE'S SWAMP.

Salad

George enjoyed having us stay in the house. Not only for the company or the cards, but for all the goodies that were showered on him. He'd never tasted Crayfish or Gummy Shark before, or a dozen other culinary delights that we introduced him to. And while we were there most of the meals were prepared by us as he went about his farm duties. Being a bachelor, a batch of scones, or a sponge cake were just plain off the menu and it pleased us no end to see him hoe into a variety of taste sensations that were rare to him. He delighted in recalling the time when, after a hard hot day on the tractor we sat him down to a beautifully prepared salad. "It was beautiful," he salivated. "I'd eaten the Virginian ham, the corned beef, the lovely accompanying salad smothered in creamy mayonnaise, and was wiping the plate with a piece of buttered rye bread when shock, horror, it revealed a crack with two chips under the dressing. They'd fed me on the bloody cat's dish."

"They fed me on the Bloody cats dish"

It wasn't only George that had to be wary. After complaining of the taste and colour of some bread, it was discovered that it had been kept on the lower shelf in the huge floor freezer. Above it was freshly killed liver and kangaroo meat which had dripped blood all over it. We also discovered that the red liquid on top of the ice cream was not strawberry topping.

George was also a master of improvisation. When one of the players during a game of cards enquired as to whether it had started to rain yet, he replied, "just a minute," and gave an ear piercing whistle. Ten seconds later the dog, Rusty, trotted in through the fly strips. "Nup," he replied, feeling that Rusty was still dry. "Not yet".

Crappy Shot

Despite the loss of an eye, George was still a great shot. He seemed to be able to drop a target a lot further out than the rest of us. I think the one eye gave him no perspective of distance, the brain only had one lens to rely on for a reference point. But he insisted that if you could distinguish colour it was within range. On a warm yet blowy autumn evening in the mid-80s, we found ourselves at the small irrigation runoff known as "Dave's Swamp", the site of Len's earlier mishap. It was a low depression at the end of some large irrigation paddocks. Probably five feet deep when full and the size of a football stadium, it filled mainly with runoff water from the surrounding crops. It was a great place for ducks to roost up during the day and come out to feed on the crops at night. Any birds that were there, took to the sky on our arrival, but

always returned of an evening if they hadn't been shot at. It was interspersed with dead trees and boxthorn on the perimeter with one sole surviving peppercorn tree just about dead centre. It was this I chose to sit under, my back against the trunk, my five shot Browning magnum across my knees. It was a magnum but I never used 3-inch magnum cartridges, 2¾ were dear enough as it was. I had a commanding view of the north-south sheet of water in front of me.

George had set up on my left at the south end of the same run, probably eighty yards away, where the water terminated. He'd selected a position central to the same north-south sheet of water that I was presiding over. (The lagoon or runoff had three sections in the shape of a clover leaf, we were on the most easterly.) The wind was howling from behind George straight up the centre towards me. He knew that if birds approached, it would be from the north end so that they could bank into the wind to land. On a howling day like this they always sought out the lee end of the water to land. Being cautious they'd settle down 40 or 50 yards out and paddle in to shore after first inspecting the surrounds. Out of the corner of my eye, to the north I sensed a movement, and there, circling in to line up for a landing, were a nice pair of grey teal, my favourite eating duck. They are succulent, easy to pluck and prepare, and not as dark or dry as a blackie. I looked to the left, wondering if George had made the same observation. There he was, crouching behind a huge log, with his pants around his ankles attending a call of nature. What was it about Dave's Swamp and the Rosses and calls of nature? Looks like it was all up to me … no reflex shooting here, I had plenty of time to think as they zoomed in without a wing beat, straight up the middle, against a howling wind and only forty-five yards out. I had them dead to rights ... I couldn't miss ... could I?

I emptied the five-shot magazine, and didn't lay a pellet on either bird. And watched in awe as George, pants still around his ankles, leaned across the log, picked up the double-barrel and dropped them both with two neat shots.

He would rubbish me good heartedly in company about that little incident for many years to come, getting lots of laughs at my expense. My only comeback was that he had a howling gale directly behind him and my eyes were watering, not from the gale, but the stench.

One Shot

George told of times as a young man. The swamp was full and ducks of all descriptions were huddled on the shoreline in their thousands. They were in mobs some forty deep and hundreds of yards long. Fisheries and Wildlife authorities had estimated a population of around 10,000 birds. An enormous mob of these had made themselves at home on the shoreline just below George's haystacks. Using the old single shot Greener, he crawled on his belly for a hundred yards, raising his head every so often to size up the situation and take a breather. Then, continuing on amongst the long grass and tussocks, he arrived at a distance that was to his liking, about forty-five yards, and stopped, lying quietly to regain his breathe. Then, carefully and ever so slowly, he raised himself to one knee, and gently set the hammer to full firing lock. The old Greener was primed with a heavy load of number-one shot

packed in a cardboard-wadded cartridge. And just before the shot was taken he yelled at the top of his voice, "Heyyyy", squeezing the trigger at the same time. He didn't aim at them but over the sitting ducks, sitting ducks indeed, heads raised because of the yell, dozens jumped into the deadly hail of shot as it raked a path through the mob.

One single shot had brought down twenty-eight birds. All were plucked, cleaned and sold to traders for a small sum. Along with rabbits and quail they were a nice supplement to a very meagre income, and helped to get them through some extremely hard times.

Chicklings

During one of these heavily populated seasons he raided a black duck's nest below the milking shed and placed half a dozen eggs under one of his broody hens. "Never," said George, "will I do that again." The chickens hatched and mum cared for them, fed them and showed them the ways of a good chook.

But every time the little rascals went near the swamp, they'd venture out into the water, swimming and dipping and playfully chasing one another while Mum was running up and down the shoreline beside herself with anxiety. She'd cluck and call and scratch, all to no avail, as the little blighters were having too much fun. And when they developed wings and flew away to explore the wide unknown, she pined for a week.

"No, never again," said George.

Punt Limbo

It was never just duck opening weekend for my brothers, myself and mates. Keen as mustard, everybody would work through the Christmas holidays of each year, to be able to take their vacation to coincide with the season's opening in March.

A good season would see us camped for up to a fortnight, combining our adventure with hunting duck, quail in season and rabbits, using the camp as a base. These activities were mostly carried out in early morning or evenings, leaving the remainder of the day to clean our bags, have a siesta, or collect bait with a view to spending a pleasant afternoon down at the river fishing. Netting yabbies from the many dams on the property provided heaps of the bait-sized crustaceans, as well as buckets full of the larger specimens which were boiled up on the campfire. Peeled and marinated in vinegar and pepper with a touch of salt, they provided succulent feasts that couldn't be matched, even by expensive restaurants in the big smoke. And they were free.

One exceptionally dry year in the early seventies saw the swamp a lot lower than normal. Still deep enough to punt, but boats were just about out of the question. If the outboard was raised a notch or two and you owned a weedless prop it could be managed, but the numerous stumps threatening to remove a propeller at every turn disheartened all but the foolhardy (or the well-off). But we did enjoy the punting experience.

The stealthy craft got us close to game, was cheap and gave us all washboard tummies ... ahh the memories. Brother John and I spent most of the previous winter constructing our punts out of marine ply and light, inch thick framework, all sealed up with fibreglass edges and camouflage paint. The craft were ready. We even shaped and constructed double-bladed paddles and smaller bat paddles for lying down. John's, which was designed a little wider than my attempt, floated and balanced well, whereas mine turned out rather unstable. Around fourteen feet long and only twenty-six inches wide (the reader can convert), it was like trying to balance a milk jug on a waterbed. But after careful thought a set of teardrop shaped stabilizers were designed and installed at the rear end which worked a treat. Talk about winged keels, Ben Lexcen would have been proud.

The punt's design also allowed for the operator to lie down and paddle on his stomach using the small bat paddles. The satisfaction that lying down flat in the punt on the mirror-like water quietly paddling was rewarding and probably therapeutic. It was enough to mesmerise the operator into dropping off into peaceful slumber, which did occur on occasion. I was rudely awoken once when the craft nosed into a dead red gum with a thump.

Misty, foggy mornings were especially enjoyable. The eerie effects thousands of ghostly trees and stumps emitted as they appeared out of the hazy gloom was amazing. The slightest sounds were enhanced by the fog as they echoed across the water. Unless you took a compass you were hopelessly lost until the sun came up, but it didn't matter, it was akin to floating through a wonderland of clouds on a waterbed. It was also hunting by sound and stealth, as once into the gloom of fog, the only indication of locating game was to home in on the chatter of teal or the raucous call of the blackie in the distance, paddle in their direction for twenty strokes, then glide to a halt and listen again, correcting as you went, slowly by stealth homing in on the quarry.

One morning Ken was doing just that, sitting up using the double-bladed paddles when out of the white gloom a fence wire appeared. The bow of the punt had already slipped under the wire when shock horror, he recognized it for what it was. To prevent George's cattle from using the exposed banks of the swamp to get to greener pastures he had installed a line of star pickets fifty yards into the water and hung an electrified fence from it.

Doing a perfectly executed backwards limbo Ken managed to slip under the zapping wire, his nose just millimetres from being hooked. "Whew," he exclaimed looking back at the hot wire, "that was close." Then, "Oh, no, where's my bloody gun?" His new automatic Browning, which had been facing backwards was missing, obviously being flipped clean out of the punt as it hit the wire. Finding his way back to the farm (ironically something he wouldn't have been able to do in the fog, without knowing the whereabouts of the wire), he announced his misfortune and we all followed him back to the fence line. George turned the power off, donned a pair of gumboots and followed, wading in to the indicated site, with a long handled three-tined pitchfork. "I'll find it," he declared, proceeding to jab and poke the muddy bottom as he advanced. "What the hell are you doing, George?" Ken blurted,

"Christ, if you find it you'll split the stock." He pointed to the second last picket, "It should be around here." Sure enough, five minutes of feeling around in the mud and there it was.

It was as good as new after a thorough cleaning and oiling, except for some welding-like burns near the muzzle.

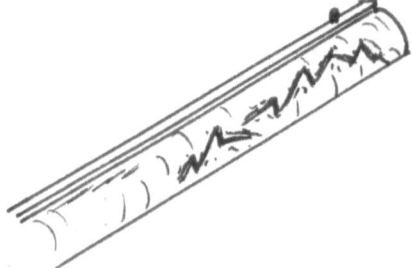

IT WAS AS GOOD AS NEW EXCEPT FOR MUZZLE BURNS.

Poor Lenny

You'd reckon Len had had enough misfortune in his life, but worse was to come. After the war he won a job at the Bendigo Foundry and continued to work there until the mid-sixties when he was just about ready to snatch it and enjoy his long service entitlement. In charge of a heavy metal press and cutter, he was instructing an apprentice with hand signals. The young fellow was operating the on/off switch of the hydraulic bender/cutter which was situated away from the machine. On the rollers was a huge slab of 3/4-inch steel plate which had to be bent. As the noise of the foundry prevented oral instructions, Len was obliged to signal the operator when enough was enough. The lad mistook Len's signal to ease off and applied full pressure. The huge plate sheared, jumping straight

Len, Joyce and George, with Guests

up off the rollers, taking Len's face with it. Poor handsome Lenny.

The steel plate sheared off his chin, his lips, his, nose and eyebrows. He was critical for some time, and for years after had to return to hospital for skin grafts, blood clots, and corrective surgery. But, as always, Len got through it. He could talk, but with a lisp. The scarring gave him a permanent harelip.

His partial nose was reshaped and ended up reasonably presentable. The eyebrows and chin were scarred and only grew patchy hair but were also tolerable. He grew a moustache to hide the lips and scrubbed up pretty well.

After an extended court hearing, he was awarded a minimal amount of money which he used to purchase a new car and caravan, and helped his son to establish a chook farm in Queensland.

Life Savers

During one especially hectic opening to the duck hunting season, I found myself wading beside a large stump one hundred yards offshore. Eyes skywards, I was firing and reloading instinctively, feeling for a cartridge in my ammunition bag and reloading automatically without looking down. A pair of hardheads approached in a long low sweep, I had them dead to rights … keep still, don't move, nearly here, now, up and swing through from behind, pass them, lead a few metres, keep swinging and fire. Click, nothing. They were gone, they didn't miss a wing beat. "What the?"

I broke the gun to discover there, in the breech, was a packet of Lifesavers, and that they were … for the ducks.

[Lifesavers, are a confectionery similar in shape and size to a shotgun cartridge.]

Spinner's Reward

As the poem says (see page 7), it wasn't that Len was tight or stingy, he hated waste, and losing spinners really pissed him off. He loved to walk, he'd walk for miles chasing game or fish. The relatively flat ground of the northern country was nothing compared to the muddy slogs of the mountain ranges of New Guinea. There he'd learnt to value everything he possessed from bully beef to bullets. And here, back home, was no different, if it had a specific use, then value it for that reason.

The section of river that meandered down from the siphon at the Macorna channel to Healy's old house, traversed through wild lignum, scrub and boxthorn and was lined with river gums and stunted Mallee trees. The many bends that afforded deep holes were named, "Joyce's Hole", "Len's Hole" and so on. Not very imaginative, but for a reason, and they knew exactly where the spot was that was mentioned. The river was just as it was 200 years ago, virtually untouched by man. Well, no evidence of it until you hit the large concrete siphon which allowed the Macorna channel to pass under the river. This section was approximately 4–5 miles in length as the wood duck flies, but if you walked the river you could double that, what with all the twists and bends.

It was a beautiful, clear, still morning in April, the heat of summer had diminished and only a waft of breeze caressed the eucalypts. Len was quietly making his way upriver. He liked to work his lures upriver as he reckoned that the fish were pointing that way in the current and his presence was not as easily revealed if he approached from behind. Not a bad theory, but not so convincing in this slow moving water. Nevertheless, there was Len, two nice redfin in the bag, sun shining through the trees, birds flitting between branches, crows calling in the distance; all was well with the world. He flicked the lure out across the wide bend above him, and paused to allow it to attain a depth where the fish might be. The hole, he estimated, was around 12 feet deep, "a good one," he thought, as it had produced nice fish in the past. But then "You bludger!" he mumbled as the lure came to an abrupt halt. For a fleeting second he imagined it might be a hit and raised the rod tip to set the hooks, but no follow up thumps or movements were evident. The lure had become entangled. "Bugger," he thought. Not only had it been a reliable lure, it had caught fish this morning, but to replace it meant a return to camp, some twenty minutes away. He relaxed the line and strolled upriver, above the snag, where he could attempt to release it at a new angle.

"Nup," no such luck, still snagged tight. There was nothing left to do but strip off and follow the line down, that or snap it off, and that wasn't going to happen. He crawled out on a log above the hole so that he could lower himself into deep water rather than bog down the steep muddy bank.

The top layer of water was beautifully warm but two feet further down it was freezing. Once in, he breaststroked across to where the line was located. A deep breath and down he went. The line crossed a sunken branch and stopped on a large prickly object. All he could do was feel his way around as the water was too dark to see anything, and what with the mud he was stirring up, there was no hope. Out of breath, back to the surface for a few seconds, then down again.

The spinner was there, he could feel it at the end of the line, but no way would it release. But would the object? He felt it roll. What if I could lift it? Back for another breath. "Christ, what a man'll do," he pondered. This time his battle plan was decided, bring the whole bloody log up and free the spinner on the bank. Down he went again. This time he got a good hold, there were holes at each end so, with legs straddling it, he pushed down with all his strength while lifting with his arms. It released in a cloud of mud. With the extra weight his legs disappeared into the bottom with each struggling step, but he was eventually able to make it to the bank. He pushed and dragged and slid it up until it was finally high and dry. To his astonishment, there in front of him was his spinner, glistening in the sun, accompanied by a hundred others. It was a roll of barbed wire that had obviously rolled off the back of a farm ute while fencing.

It had been accumulating lures and spinners of all descriptions for years, who knows how long? It looked like a bloody Christmas tree, he thought. He forgot all about his cold shivering and muddy body, as he detached lure after lure and popped them in his game bag. So pleased was he with his good fortune, after releasing all the lures he threw the roll back in the newly named "Spinner Hole", and would revisit it every so often.

The Frog

There were times, early in the piece, when George had as many as three nice cod tethered down at the Loddon, some over forty pounds. It was the mid-1930s, work was hard to get and food a little harder. The heat of summer prevented any hope of keeping game or fish fresh for any length of time, and the kerosene fridge would only hold so much. So the tethering method kept the catch alive and fresh for weeks. Heavy fishing line was passed through a slit in the lower jawbone and tied off to a suitable anchor point. George liked to select a spot in the river above a good submerged log or stump. Just enough line was left to allow the fish to swim back and shelter under such protection.

Despite the restraint the fish didn't seem to have any detrimental effects and continued to feed, though in a restricted search area. To those in the big smoke it seemed a cruel act to perpetrate on a helpless fish, but as he used to say, "It's alright for them to complain, they have a shop on every bloody corner, and we've got nothing." This was food for the whole family and when its number was up we'd all have a decent meal for a change, one does get sick of duck and rabbit.

The Loddon, in those pre-European carp days, was as clear as a bell, except after heavy rain or flooding. Even then it only took a week or so to clear up. One could peer into the crystal clear water and observe fish and other native water life going about their business in long green weed and waving stands of river grass. The carp, introduced in later years, were soon to turn many rivers into weedless, muddy environments that ruined the native fish's habitat.

Weed and grass-lined bottoms which housed shrimp and yabbies and small fish disappeared and, with the food chain broken, many of these legendary fish vanished. Only in recent years with the hard work of environmental groups and government bodies, and a restocking program, have we seen a slight return to these times. The carp still remain a big problem.

George fished the river regularly, even at times resorting to "square hooks" when things got desperate. "Square hook" is the colloquial term for the illegal drum net. This was a large roll of chicken wire, or better still, small holed weldmesh, formed into the shape of a 44-gallon drum. Sometimes over four feet long and two feet six inches wide. The ends were filled in with tapered cones of the same material leading to the central drum with an opening large enough to allow entry of a decent sized fish. So the only access for fish feeding upriver was via the conical opening of the square hook, where they would become trapped until bagged.

It was always located in a narrow channel between obstructions, near submerged logs and stumps with the main opening facing down current. It was placed where a fish might swim to gain access to feeding grounds upstream, the theory being that fish mainly feed upriver from their normal residence. This would allow them a quick exit from danger with the aid of a downward current. Fish, when caught angling, always used the current to run downstream, so the reasoning was logical. Finally, the net was placed deep enough so as not to alert authorities of its presence. The only means of retrieval was a stout length of fencing wire, or a grappling hook. No obvious signs of its whereabouts would be left visible, or the jig was up.

One had to be totally aware of current weather forecasts and the rise and fall of the river level. If the river rose, the net could not be retrieved. If it dropped it became visible to authorities policing the river, or worse, thieving bloody poachers who'd steal the catch. On one visit the author and friends came upon a drum net partially submerged after a drop in the river. Over seventy pounds of yellowbelly and redfin were inside.

George mostly just loved to sit and fish. To sit quietly on the bank under the shade of a eucalyptus tree with a rod resting on a forked stick, and a pipe in his hand, now that was pure bliss for George. How many times while fishing had he witnessed nature's performances unfolding before him? Huge mobs of wood duck (or maned goose) would appear from nowhere calling out their familiar cat-like meowing call as they flew past. Sometimes, unaware of his presence, skimming to a halt on the sheet of water directly in front of him. They preferred to roost during the day on the river and come out to feed on the local crops at night, gorging themselves until the local farmers, inspecting their investments in the morning, shooed them off.

Deadly tiger snakes slithered from their protective retreats to sunbake in the early morning's warmth. Once he witnessed a young fox, stealthily foraging amongst the tussocks and boxthorn on the opposite side of the river. After a small commotion it emerged from some lignum with a hare in its jaws that wasn't much smaller than the fox. It was kicking and writhing with all its might in a vain attempt to escape. And it nearly did so, until a much larger adult appeared from nowhere and together they subdued the hapless prey. There was always something to occupy or entertain, and he loved it.

Local bait was plentiful. Any dam they wished to try provided yabbies by the bucketful. The river abounded in large shrimp, some large enough to give a painful nip, and earthworms could always be had by simply digging beside the channel bank, or better still, the hosings from the milking shed was alive with large worms. The green tree frog was always available under tree bark beside the river.

It was one of these that George had selected as bait just on dusk one evening. He fashioned a rod-rest from a forked branch and carefully rigged a float with the frog suspended about three feet below the surface. He gently pierced the hook through a pinched fold of skin and lowered it into the river. A frog swimming in circles under a float must attract a worthwhile catch, and a self-motivated lure was much better than a stationary one. Every so often he would check the float's whereabouts by cautiously flicking the torch light across the water, ensuring that the slow current had not jagged it on a stump or sucked it under a log.

Close to an hour had elapsed with no action whatsoever, and the torch was played across the water in search of the float. There was the float, and cheerfully perched on top was the green tree frog, completely out of harm's way, and croaking his mating song

for all the world to hear, hook and line still attached.

Admiring his ingenuity, George displayed a gentler side. He reeled in the line, gently unhooked the brave little amphibian, and placed him under a sheet of loose bark on the same tree he was so rudely snatched from earlier. He appreciated its survival instinct so much that from that time onward, he never ever used a frog for bait again.

Over the years there were many more incidents and stories to tell. There were fishing trips to the Murray, the Darling and Edwards rivers. We even took George to Lake Dartmouth for a week once. That really shook him, driving in the mountainous country, with vertical drops of hundreds of yards; but he loved the lake.

Occasionally I'd meet Len shopping in Lansell Plaza, Bendigo. Joyce had passed on and he'd met another nice lady, "Joyce, mark two", he'd say. We'd have a cuppa together and reminisce of the good old times. He died in 2008 at the age of 87 years. I wouldn't mind betting that if there's a heaven, the first thing he would have said to George was, "I've beaten you again." George passed away five years earlier in May 2003 at the age of 86 years.

George was more than just a great friend; he was a huge chunk of all the lives that knew him. A kind, quiet, thoughtful, decent man with a devilish sense of humour. Sadly missed, but all who met him were better for so doing.

The Insides of Old Perc

I suppose old Perc was what you might call a hypochondriac. No matter what ailment he seemed to have at the time, he always fancied it to be worse than it really was. A mild headache would most certainly develop into a brain tumour. Strained chest muscles from lifting all those bloody great fence posts around were definitely symptoms of an imminent heart attack. Yet he still managed to attain his mature years without so much as a few common colds and a broken bone or two. There wasn't too much wrong with his eyesight either, he could still plink a rabbit behind the eyes at eighty yards. There was a time when he could consistently manage the same feat thirty or forty yards further out, but since turning forty the range seemed to reduce by ten yards or so a decade.

Those distances didn't matter all that much with night shooting, as most bunnies were dispatched at forty yards or less. So it was still well within Perc's limits to continue as the shot man on the hunt.

Bill drove the 4-wheel-drive ute, he knew the terrain like the back of his hand and was able to negotiate the forested land and rocky outcrops as easily as the paddock country and on the darkest of nights was always able to return to the south boundary fence. Graham worked the spotlight, not only because of his ability to home in on a target, be it rabbit, fox or feral cat, and hold it steady without spooking the quarry, but mainly, especially on these cold nights, he enjoyed the warmth the spot radiated onto his hands.

The three mates had worked each other's properties systematically for many years, but the rabbit problem remained a constant worry, despite their regular efforts. Soil erosion was a major result and reparation a major expense. Both Perc's mates retained a devilish sense of humour, and practical jokes were always on the cards. Not too regular though, the element of surprise always returned a better response.

Graham once set up a mock rabbit in the hills during daylight hours. He knew just where to play the spot and the result was magnificent. It was constructed of small balloons partially filled with flour. It even had paper ears, thanks to some creative work from his niece; she cleverly finished it off with craft paints.

When Perc's bullet smacked into the target the "rabbit" virtually blew up in a cloud of white smoke and vanished before his disbelieving eyes. His astonished reaction pleased his mates no end.

They'd experienced better evenings for spotlighting, in fact it was downright miserable. The night air was freezing and intermittent showers met the group as they made their way up a long quartz-strewn slope that fringed the tree line. Rabbits, being smarter than humans, were scarce, preferring to nestle in the cosy warmth of their burrows, rather than brave the elements. Still, Perc had been able to eradicate nine of the blighters without a single miss; all neat head shots. He took pride in the fact that the kill was neat, clean and instant and the carcass was unblemished for the table. What they didn't keep for themselves was sold to the local butcher, as there was a ready market for "underground mutton". A better night would most likely have seen as many as thirty hanging on the rack.

Bill hadn't contributed to their comfort much by purposely guiding the 4WD under low-hanging branches, showering them with icy water. "Sorry," he'd say, but they knew he didn't mean it as the chuckle that followed always gave him away. When a complaint was screamed out, he'd reply "I can't hear you fellas, I've got the heater on full blast." Yet he always heard the order to stop, because that meant another quarry. Perc had been complaining of a stomach upset for most of the evening, and the last straw eventuated when Bill decided to negotiate a deeply ripped paddock crossways over the corrugations. "That'll do me fellas, let's call it a night," he bellowed. "It's alright for you bastards, but I think I've got a stomach ulcer that's about to burst."

The usual procedure was to stop near a large dam which was surrounded by forest at the base of a low line of quartzy hills. Firewood was collected, a small campfire lit, and the distasteful task of skinning, gutting and washing up in the dam water carried out. Halfway through the gutting process Perc's cramps became worse, and with a painful groan, he lurched forward for the toilet paper which was stashed behind the front seat, grabbed the torch and shuffled off into the darkness to answer an overpowering call of nature.

Bill, not one to miss an opportunity seized a long-handled posthole shovel from the back of the ute, scooped up a pile of rabbit guts and followed Perc's torchlight into the bush.

The rain had softened the leaves and ground-cover, making stealth easy, and under the increasing howl of an approaching squall he positioned himself behind the squatting figure, where he gently lowered the contents of the shovel onto what was once the contents of Perc. He retraced his steps to the flickering fire where both men had great difficulty in containing themselves, and waited expectantly. An ear piercing shriek and a howl of dismay carried through the night as Perc appeared, stumbling into the red glow of the campfire, clutching his stomach, and his pants still not belted up. "Quick fellas, get me to a bloody hospital, I'm fair dinkum this time, I've just lost half me guts," he blurted, panic stricken.

He couldn't understand why they rolled about in laughter at his plight, and it took a hell of a lot of convincing. He never really forgave them. Well, not until he got his revenge ... but that's another story.

The Garden Postal Chute

Thirty-seven. That's how many I'd counted. The previous year had only seen a handful, but what with another year of maturity production was underway in earnest. The parrots had beaten me then, chewing and nibbling chunks out of the entire crop long before they had ripened. But this time I'd purchased a heap of strong bird netting and felt comfortable in the knowledge that the entire tree was now enveloped in a protective white web. I had salivated for weeks in anticipation, waiting for the apricots to ripen. I watched as the green skin graduated through yellow and orange with a tinge of red on the sunny side, like an infant's blushing cheeks. A week or so and they'd be ready. A pre-taste-test with an early ripener was all that I had expected, a shock of sweet flesh exploded in my mouth, delicious, tasty and succulent.

During the final week, first duty before breakfast was to peruse the veggie patch for rabbits or hares, or any other of the multitude

of hungry invaders that might be lurking in the area. What with the worst drought in living memory, my little Garden of Eden was a magnet to all and sundry. A family of magpies didn't surprise me as I regularly supplied them damp bread which they tore apart noisily. The parents feeding the new fledglings to capacity, and then stashing the remainder for later use in a dozen different hidey holes in the rose mulch, under the park bench, even in the mower's catcher.

A few days later, I ventured through the small orchard with a view to inspect the progress of the apricot tree. This was in the furthest corner of the orchard which consisted of pear, apple, plum, peach, nectarine, olive, blood orange and even a plumcot, all of which were bearing fruit in abundance, but none nearing maturity … except the apricot of course. There, to my dismay, my inspection revealed only five of my precious apricots remained. "What the? How the? You rotten little." Disbelief and dismay flooded over me. Could it be possums? How could any bird or animal plunder my fruit right under my nose without being observed?

The following morning revealed all. At six-thirty, armed with binoculars I perused the orchard from the kitchen window, scanning the grounds, the trees, the boundary fence, even the surrounding bush, keeping the entire shebang under surveillance. Apart from some beautiful superb wrens, a willy wagtail and the magpie family, nothing else could be seen. No possums, no wallabies, no wombats. Surely koalas didn't eat apricots; they also inhabited the surrounding bush. But then, a movement, a rustling of leaves, caught my attention. It was up inside the tree in question, which was completely encased in white bird mesh, it was even tied off at the base. Tutankhamen would have been proud.

More movement, and there she was, Mrs Magpie helping herself. I watched, enchanted by her remarkable ingenuity and initiative. She had entered through a small opening in the base making her way to the top and had proceeded to remove each fruit with a deft twist, then hurling it against the inside of the netting which created a delivery chute that directed the prize all the way to the bottom where it exited through the narrow opening with a plop.

There, waiting expectantly, was her delighted family, dad and the kids, who devoured the delicacy with great endeavour, to finish and peer patiently upwards for the next delivery. Just like the mail chute down at the post office.

What could I do but admire her work and plan for a more secure containment next year.

Australian Magpie
Cracticus tibicen

Trapper Jack

As a young bloke in 1963, I found myself legally able to drink a beer, obtain a driver's licence and shoot a gun. Unlike most of my teenage mates and acquaintances at the time, alcohol wasn't all that important to me, it took years for me to develop a taste for beer. Possibly a contributing factor in my tardy acceptance of a grog was the fact that my best mate at the time Alwen "Stick" Parker, crashed his Customline head-on into a tram near the Astor Theatre, Windsor (a southern suburb of Melbourne), killing himself and his teenage passengers. Eighteen years old. What a waste.

The freedom that the possession of a motor vehicle provided was like heaven to me. To have the means at my fingertips to be able to escape the concrete and glass, and the tedious boredom of suburban life, for the huge open expanses and clean fresh air of the Victorian bush, was a regular weekend occurrence and a wonderful gift. The thrill of exploration was enough to have the camping gear packed, food, rifle and fishing rods, and point the '48 Ford Mercury anywhere as long as the big smoke was behind me. Just follow my nose, explore with no preconceived destination. To give the reader some idea of how relaxed gun laws were in those days, prior to my obtaining a driver's licence I would satisfy my hunting desires by slinging my single shot Lithgow rifle over my shoulder, and catch the number 6 Glen Iris tram into Melbourne from Prahran, where I would alight and walk through the city to Spencer Street railway station.

There I would catch the train that passed through Diggers Rest. Only on one occasion was I confronted by a Police Officer, and as long as the bolt was safely tucked away in my back pocket there were no problems. I was advised that it might be a good idea to conceal the rifle in a gun sheath or wrap it up in newspaper, so as not to startle commuters. School cadets lumped 303 rifles around all the time in those days, so it was no big deal.

Once on the train, which was only two carriages long, I could actually converse with the driver whose driving compartment was in with the passengers. About 30 kilometres out he would slow the train to a crawl and I would alight and hike across paddocks to the deep gorge east of the Calder Highway. (By the way, that's the only place I've shot a rabbit under the chin. While sighting up a bunny 60 yards below me on one of the steep slopes of the gorge, I squeezed the trigger. The bullet hit the ground below the quarry and ricocheted up into its jaw.)

After a day's hunting I'd find myself back at the railway track at a predetermined time to flag the train down; with two or three fresh rabbits, a couple for me and always one for the driver. Home was achieved the same way … with a couple of dead rabbits in the bag. I even hitchhiked back one day, in the rain, along the Calder. Could the reader ever imagine a driver stopping these days to give a stranger a lift – with a rifle and a couple of bunnies – not likely.

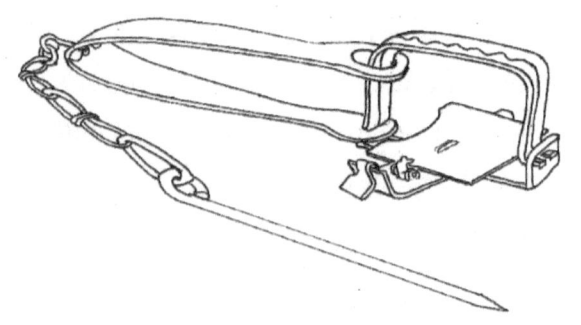

But I digress ... back to the Ford Mercury.

On one of my exploratory sorties to the north-western Mallee district I met and befriended a professional trapper in the Birchip area named Jack.

His invitation to accompany him during the trap-setting hours, starting in the early afternoon, was accepted with glee. Two hundred traps would go down in an afternoon, a most tiring assignment. The properties in the district that required Jack's services were spread far and wide and, many miles, numerous gates and dozens of rises were traversed during the operation. He was a big man, with huge forearms and could set a rabbit trap by prising the jaws open by hand, holding them open with one hand while setting the trigger with the other. Lesser beings set them by sitting them on the ground and holding the jaws apart with a foot placed on the spring, but not Jack. After some effort I acquired the art, but could only manage ten or so before my arm seized up.

Accompanying Jack on his rounds had its advantages. I was able to eradicate the odd bunny or fox that we surprised during daylight hours. I learned how to set a trap correctly. Covering the pressure plate with newspaper to prevent grit from fouling the mechanism, and gently smoothing out the run with a leafy branch, and a handful of crushed droppings to disguise the human odour, all was ready.

I also learned during collection of said catch that it was preferable to bag your own rather than purchase a shop-dressed rabbit. It was not unusual to have a rabbit baking in the hot sun for hours before its collection was achieved. Any mauled by foxes or birds of prey were still processed for the freezer. Even those with myxomatosis were included for human consumption.

A most distasteful story reached Jack's ears one morning. After helping him clear the traps we delivered them to the mobile freezer, and returned to his home for lunch, a small farmlet northwest of town.

The phone rang and Jack answered. He listened intently, nodding occasionally, then hung up. He turned and asked, "Wanna come for a ride, mate?" "Sure," I replied, "where to?" "Just gotta put a small matter right in town, won't be long."

The trip into town was decidedly quiet, and Jack's firmly set jaw convinced me not to pursue the subject. We pulled up outside the hotel and as he exited the ute he ordered, "Stay here, I'll call you if I need you." I'd never seen him so resolute or focused. He was usually so carefree, happy and jovial. But something bad was in the wind; I could sense there was definitely trouble brewing.

A couple of minutes elapsed and then raised voices and cursing emanated from the pub. Suddenly, Jack appeared in the doorway, holding by the scruff of his shirt collar, a man nearly as large as himself, but about ten years younger. He hurled him onto the pavement and set upon this unfortunate fellow like a thrashing machine, raining blows with his ham-like fists to any exposed

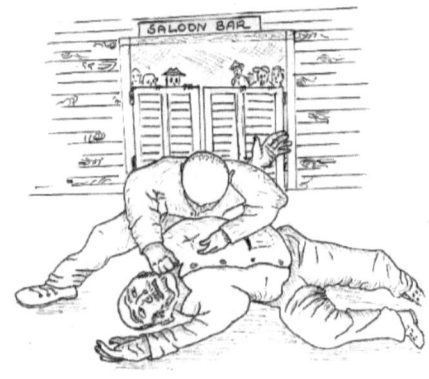

portion of the bloke that came within range.

Patrons poured from the pub and levered the two men apart. Actually, they levered Jack aside, as the recipient wasn't really up to doing much at all. "Get outa here, Jack," a man with an apron yelled, "before Alby gets here". Alby turned out to be the local law officer. Jack didn't hurry. Dusting himself off, he sauntered over to the car and said, slightly puffed, "Slide over mate, you drive." I wasn't about to argue. Doing what I was told, we drove from town and on reaching the outer limits I finally summoned up the courage to ask the obvious question. "What in friggin' hell was all that about? Jesus you nearly killed the poor bastard?"

"Poor bastard be buggered," said Jack. "That prick's been begging me for years to sell him one of the litter of Suzie's last pups. Reluctantly, we gave him first choice and he picked the strongest, best looking, lovable labrador in the litter, and he swore he'd treat him with kindness and be a good master. The bastard visited the pub last night and got so pissed he forgot that he'd tied the pup to the rear of his truck. When he arrived home, some ten miles later, there was only a pulpy pile of bloodied fur on the end of the leash. The poor little bugger must have run till his legs gave out and was then pulverized to death by the road."

Jack never heard any more about the beating.

Business Partners

After another successful trip to Jack's place, my brother Ken and I had cleaned up the catch, gutting skinning and rinsing a dozen bunnies and were heading back to the big smoke. After helping Jack with his traps we had spent till the early hours spotlighting, followed by a restless catnap in the Mercury until dawn broke. As we couldn't be bothered setting up the stove and camping gear for breakfast, we hit the road with intentions of eating at the first opportunity.

The rising sun flickered through a thousand trees lining the left hand shoulder of the road, mesmerising both driver and passenger alike. No traffic and the monotony of straight roads had us both semi-dozing, being lulled into a fantasy world of flickering lights and a purring V8 motor; we had to stop.

Half an hour down the road a truck stop came into view. It was obvious the food was good as the patronage of parked big wheelers out the front was testament to the popularity of the place. If the truckers stopped there, the food and service was a moral to be good. "This'll do us," said Ken. "Let's have a break and get some tucker into us, I'm starving." So was I.

We entered the cafeteria section, which boasted an open fireplace and the old fashioned high-backed slide-in seating on both sides of a laminated table, effectively making each table a private booth. At the wall end was a console of selections of latest hits all available at the press of a button.

We each selected a slap-up breakfast of bacon, sausages, eggs, tomatoes and onions, all on toast, washed down with a large pot of tea that provided two cups each.

Well satisfied, our hunger pangs gone, and still the prospect of at least two hours more to drive, Ken nodded to the proprietor to provide the bill. "Hope you enjoyed your breakfast," he offered, placing the written bill face down on the table. "Fantastic," said Ken, as he rolled one side of the bill over, peeking like a professional gambler inspecting a poker hand.

The man was nearly back behind the counter when Ken called, "Excuse me." He glanced back to see Ken beckoning him back to the table. "Yes, can I help you?" he quizzed, retracing his steps to our booth. This is when I felt like crawling under the table, this man was used to handling truckers, a couple of blow-in hunters would be child's play. "I was just wondering," said Ken, "if there was any discount for someone in the same business?" His face lit up, "Oh, you have a restaurant?" he answered with a smile. "No", said Ken, bluntly. "I'm a bloody burglar, this bill is outrageous."

The owner's eyes met mine, cringing and trapped at the wall end of the booth. I rolled my eyes and shrugged with a smile trying to

portray the image that it was all a joke and all was well. "We hang burglars around here," he offered, and shuffled back to the counter, behind which hung a shotgun above the head of a huge wild boar.

Images came to mind of me and Ken up on the wall beside the gory trophy with the inscription, "Paid the Price", on the engraved brass nameplate. "Move," I said, trying to push Ken off the seat. "Let me out. If you're not in the car by the time I pay this bill I'm leaving without you."

Approaching the cashier, I paid, and when I arrived Ken was there in the vehicle, with the motor running. The truck stop never looked so good ... in the rear vision mirror.

Spotting Rats

Around 1957, My good mates Joe and Ross and I discovered the Richmond abattoirs and the landfill and tip directly opposite. The abattoirs were like a huge stockyard complex that sorted and directed the beasts for killing into the various pens. We never got to see the finished product, they must have been processed elsewhere. Either that or we weren't permitted into that area. Post and rail corrals guided the animals into concrete killing pens where the primitive and cruel methods of dispatching the unfortunate animals were carried out. My ghoulish mates guided me into the pig slaughter pen with the words, "you've gotta check this out, it's awesome." Awesome it was ... I experienced bad dreams for ages, bearing witness to the pain and suffering these animals endured. And it wasn't only pigs. Beautiful, young brown-eyed calves were subjected to the same treatment. As many as twenty beasts were herded into the concrete pen of four foot high solid walls and a floor which sloped to the centre drain.

A gumboot-clad man entered the pen armed only with a sledgehammer and proceeded to smash each animal with one blow just above and between the eyes. An inaccurate blow not only disfigured the animal but prolonged its suffering, the recipient falling to the floor in shivering death throes. But the worst memory for me was the squealing. The remaining animals, witness to their mate's misfortune, would squeal in terrified fright, shivering in anticipation of their coming fate. How can man do this to an innocent animal I thought, no chance of escape, no hope of reprieve? My thoughts recalled those flickery newsreels of the prison camps in WWII.

Boars too large to wallop with a hammer were humanely put down with a 22 bullet. Why weren't the rest handled like that? It must have been too much expense.

As the darkness of night descended we rode our bikes to the Richmond tip opposite the abattoirs. There must have been a huge amount of offal dumped there as the stench was unbelievable. Why would we want to visit such a place? The hunting. Living in the tip were hordes of the largest rats we'd ever seen, some as big as small cats. It started with stone throwing, not very successfully, but then Ross produced an old Gecado air rifle, this tipped the odds our way and was a heap of fun.

As the night drew nearer, we would take turns spotlighting rats. A bicycle was turned upside down while one of the group operated the pedals. This in turn rotated the dynamo, which provided the power to the lights. This was our Sony PlayStation and it was real. The Gecado was a great air rifle, accurate and reliable. Combined with Blackboy pellets, a soft lead projectile that had a larger than normal air pocket at the rear with no narrow waist (unlike the pellets on sale today), accuracy could be relied on up to forty yards or more. We amused ourselves for hours on that stinking tip, eradicating rats by the score. I think the South Eastern Freeway now covers the site.

Look Up to Your Peeers

Joe's father Horace was a war hero, having been awarded the *Croix de Guerre* by the French government for gallantry in action during World War I. He was also awarded the DSM by the Australian Government. Horace was a lovely man, reminding me of the actor Gary Cooper. Tall, with a similar build, he was a quiet man with always a good word and smile.

One Guy Fawkes Night someone blew up Horace's letterbox with a penny bunger and Joe approached Ross and me to exact revenge.

[Author's note: Guy Fawkes Night was a celebration held to commemorate the capture and arrest of Guy Fawkes, a member of the Gunpowder Plot in November 1605. He was guarding a huge store of explosives set to go off under the House of Lords, and was intending to kill the king, James the first. He and his fellow conspirators were executed a month later in January 1606. It was held every November, until the authorities declared that it was too dangerous.]

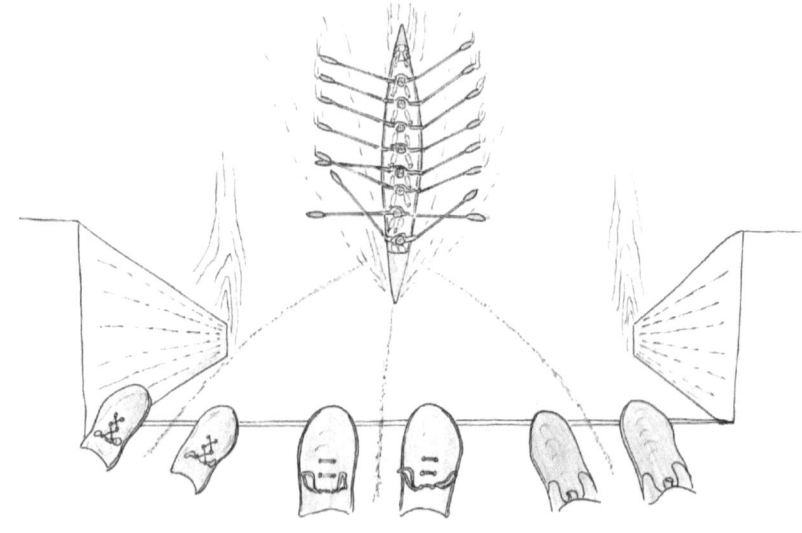

We looked forward to the celebration as we got to let off skyrockets and Catherine wheels and penny- and twopenny-bungers and a dozen other exotically named fireworks. From a high vantage point on the fifth of November, sky rockets could be seen all over the Melbourne suburban skyline. Also, the odd house burnt down.

Joe had discovered the culprits were an older boy, Alby, and his twin brother Thomas, both of whom attended school at Burnley College, a school renowned for catering to the well-to-do, situated on the banks of the Yarra River. Both boys were members of the rowing team which would stay on after school hours to practice on the river. Ross had discovered through a contact the time and boat they were to use. Many times we had collected pigeons and eggs from the underside of the Church Street Bridge and were familiar with the access route that would take us to the precarious middle of the bridge.

The ledges around the vertical columns were only about four inches wide but if one was to balance and stretch for a hold on the corner one could inch across the underside of the bridge. This was an adrenalin rush as the slightest slip would find us plummeting thirty feet to the river below. The slippery pigeon poop added another element of peril to the climb. Four o'clock. The three mates had made it safely to the centre pylon as the practice sculls were taking to the river. We watched and waited while the activity increased. Locating Alby and Thomas was easy as their red hair stood out like beacons in the long rowboat. Eight boys and a cox all in a line, heading straight for our ambush. Each one of us had sculled a large amount of water before our rendezvous on the bridge, and were all busting by the time the rowers arrived. It was like an old cowboy movie. "Steady, wait for it, steady, not yet, wait till you see the whites of their eyes." They were nearly upon us, "let em have it." How could we miss, three streams of piss cascaded down on the hapless rowers, there was no escape, it was hard enough to turn one of those rowing shells when boys weren't pissing on you, let alone now. Even the cox was showered. Come to think of it, he probably got the worst of it as he held a trumpet-like loudspeaker pointing up in the air. Their rhythm completely shattered, oars and arms flailed everywhere, the boat glided to an abrupt halt against the side of a pylon. Our escape was disadvantaged by the difficulty factor of trying to descend a hazardous climb while laughing your head off.

Threats and cursing echoed from the water, repercussions might have been harsh if our identities were discovered, but we all agreed, revenge was sweet. Alby and Thomas knew it was us but didn't want to rat for fear that their own misdemeanours might be disclosed. All square, 15-all.

Underground Adventures

Just below the Church Street Bridge in Richmond is an exit to a stormwater tunnel complex. A present day gang have apparently taken over this area as a rendezvous and hideout and, according to a television report on the subject done a few years ago, claim to be the discoverers of all that the underground complex can give. Sorry fellas, we were doing that 55 years ago, and probably others before us. Joe, Ross and I, with torches, drinks and food, would enter the drain, which, from memory, was about twenty feet across, and we'd travel underground for miles through many different Melbourne suburbs including South Yarra, Prahran, Armadale and Malvern. Walking miles underground with feet straddling the constant stream of water that meandered down the centre was no mean feat, especially for the hips. Our echoes resounded off the brick-lined tunnels, and distant faint mysterious noises emanating from the darkness ahead gave us a constant adrenalin rush.

All this was exceeded only by the discovery of new and exciting challenges ahead in the gloom. Interconnecting tunnels, and underground waterfalls, beside which steel ladders gave us access to the next level. Not to mention rats and bats. The further we entered, the smaller the tunnels became, requiring the need to stoop, or in extreme cases, to crawl. Sometimes a crossroad of connecting tunnels required the scientific calculation of paper, scissors, or rock, to determine in which direction we would venture.

We located what we thought was the drain that led from the Alfred Hospital which emitted that distinct disinfectant odour.

Another led to the Prahran Market, and if we were adventurous enough, a street drain grill in the gutter outside the market could be reached by crawling on hands and knees down a small pipe that emptied into the main outlet. There, in turn, as access was only available to us one at a time, we were able to lie on our backs and observe the activity in the street above, and there Joe discovered a dastardly new use for a water pistol. Many a young lady must have thought they were incontinent.

In Armadale, a ladder was located which reached above us to a grid of speckled light thirty feet above. Hand over hand I scaled the ladder only to find that it terminated at a round street grid that was stuck tight and couldn't be opened. A man washing a '47 Chevy Stylemaster got the shock of his life when a voice emanated from the ground. "Wouldn't have the time would you mate?" I enquired.

I could see him through the grill, he turned, looked around and returned to his task. Again I asked, "How's the time going, mate?" Again he turned, this time doing a complete circle, shook his head and resumed the job. The third occasion was the last straw, he threw the sponge in the bucket with a sudsy splash and bellowed, "There's either someone there or I'm going bloody mental, where the frigging hell are you?" "Down here, mate" I replied from the drain. "Jesus, are you alright?" he enquired, "Can I get help?" I assured him all was okay and he advised us that we were in a dead end street in Armadale. "You fella's better get the hell outa there, there's rain coming in a few hours." "What are you washing your car for then?" I queried. "Don't be a smartarse and get going," he ordered gruffly. By the time we retraced our footsteps back to the Richmond exit the rain was falling. An hour later, the complex of tunnels was enveloped in a foaming, swirling, cascading express of rainwater thundering through everything in its path and emptying into the Yarra River in a foaming white dump of whirlpools. We never ventured there again without checking the weather forecast.

The Snack

It was 1983 and our Victorian prospecting club had organized a three thousand kilometre expedition to the Western Australian gold fields. Val was one of thirteen members who dreamt of finding the big one, and had agreed to join my party of three to share costs for the entire trip of six weeks. The plan was to allow a week's travel to Kalgoorlie, four weeks solid prospecting and a week to return. Our co-traveller was George, an ex-plumbing Teacher from Richmond Technical School. A lovely bloke who wasn't experiencing the best of health. The trip coincided with him receiving results from a test his doctor had organized just prior to leaving. He thought, "Bugger it. It may be my last opportunity to experience a trip like this." So he signed up, with a view to being advised of the results en route.

We should have woken up earlier, but it didn't take all that long to discover that Val might have been a bad choice as travelling companion. The first indication being that she refused to go along with our plan of having an expenses pool. Our idea was for all to deposit, say $500 each, in our travelling moneybox and draw from it as required. Fuel and costs, as they presented themselves, to be paid from the kitty, with any remainder divided up at the end of the trip. "No," she said, "if you purchase fuel, I'll pay one third on the spot. What if George or you wants a hamburger and I only want fries? I've lost out." We tried to explain that it only applied to travel expenses, personal stuff like food, smokes or alcohol was your own responsibility. We found out at the end of the expedition why she felt this way.

The dual cab Hilux and trailer were packed to the brim,

including all of the rear seat, leaving only the front for seating. This meant that the centre passenger had to straddle the gear stick. "I'm, having the window seat," she declared. "No way is the driver reaching between my legs to change gear." "Don't worry," said George, "he wouldn't want to." That started the first bad blood. Then we discovered she had her own tent packed away in her parcel of goodies. At every evening camp she had her modern sleeping quarters up and ready in three minutes, and was inside imbibing her private stash of whiskey before we had even driven the tent pegs in.

We ended up preferring this arrangement, but the fact remained that she hadn't informed us of her camping arrangements at the start, and I had catered for an extra stretcher and other stuff which we carted around for 7000 kilometres for nothing. George and I carried out normal conversations as friends do on all subjects, whereas Val only opened up when it suited her, not bothering to participate in any of our congenial chit chat. If we joined the rest of the party for a sit down restaurant meal (which were few and far across the Nullarbor) Val would excuse herself and dine privately. We finally concluded that she was just plain stingy. When invited to share some scrambled eggs for breakfast, she declared, "I would never eat anything out of an animal's bottom."

Further proof of her stinginess came some 200 kilometres north of Kalgoorlie, during a relocation of camp sites. "Stop the car, stop the car," she screamed. I jammed on the brakes nearly jack-knifing the trailer, and pulled up in a cloud of red dust. "What have I hit?" I queried, worrying that someone or something was lying bleeding back on the track. She dived out of the passenger door and disappeared into the dust behind the vehicle, followed by George. Twenty seconds passed and George appeared at the passenger door, with eyes rolling. "You're not gonna believe this, mate." Behind him Val waddled up, a huge grin on her face. Clutched between her folded arms were five refundable soft drink bottles. "You've got to be kidding," I blurted. "You've jeopardized a collision with the convoy behind, for fifty bloody cents." Underneath I was saying, "You stupid, stingy, money hungry bitch."

After a hard day's prospecting the group gathered together around a communal camp fire, to relate the day's activities, and compare nuggets. Toasted crumpets, even marshmallows, and shared drinks made each night a happy amiable affair. Val would present herself to the group very relaxed, having had her own personal session in her tent, never sharing or participating, although she would accept and scoff down any crumpets that were offered to her. At a place called Bummers Creek, as the camp stirred one beautifully serene morning, I was cooking the breakfast bacon. George and half a dozen others were warming themselves around the campfire as the billy boiled on the stainless fire grill. Val's tent zip opened with a flourish and out she stepped, stretched yawning, and approached the group.

Despite my encouragement, George and Val hadn't engaged in much conversation at all since the first day, and much to my surprise, he initiated a response. "Morning Val," he greeted her cordially. Showing her surprise at his greeting, she returned. "Oh, yes, good morning George." I thought, "That's nice, maybe we are at a turning point here, things are looking up." Then George offered, "I had a dream about you last night, Val." Even more surprised, she raised an eyebrow and smiled, "You had a dream about me?" she queried. Interested observers listened intently, this was going to be a revelation. "Yes," he replied, "I dreamt that you were a circus and every one was getting in for free".

"You bastard," she screamed, chasing him around the camp fire and hurling lumps of quartz in his direction, while the rest of us rolled with uncontrollable laughter. It did break the ice for a while, though not for long.

We relocated to a place called Niagara, the exact opposite of the famous place, hot dry and dusty. One of the party had bumped into a professional prospector who was working a surface claim only walking distance from our new camp. He was a nice fellow named John and, being alone for months at a time, he craved company and enjoyed immensely our evening campfire get-togethers.

John had invited us to detect his surface claim, not being particularly worried about any of us scavenging the odd nugget on the surface. He was working a large dry-blowing patch to a depth of around six feet, feeding the motorized dry-blower with a bobcat.

A group of us were lounging around one morning on John's

machinery having a yarn with him after a morning's detecting. Val, approaching the crest of a nearby rise, caught sight of us all together and sauntered down to say hello to John, and catch up on any new finds that may have come to light. On arriving she unbuckled her detector harness, dropped her pick and bag and settled down on a pile of separated quartz.

"How'd you go, Val," John enquired, "any nuggets?" She smiled back, "No nuggets."

And then, pleased as punch, "But I did have a lovely feed of sandalwood nuts." (Sandalwood nuts are an Australian native nut encased in a hard shell, tasting much like a small version of a walnut, about the size of a child's marble, very tasty and more-ish.) "Oh," said John, "you found a sandalwood tree full of nuts". "No," she replied, "I was detecting a few gullies away and came upon a large pile of them just lying on the ground. So I sat down and

SANDALWOOD

gorged myself." He smiled knowingly and gave a chuckle. "What?" she answered. "Oh, nothing," said John.

She was getting agitated, "NO, come on. What?" "Well," he replied thoughtfully. "If you found them in a heap with no tree visible, then they have more than likely passed through an emu. The large birds can't digest them and crap them out in a pile."

Roars of laughter enveloped the group and Val almost turned blue. She wouldn't even eat eggs.

After a 100 kilometre trip to civilization, for provisions, George received word of his test results. He was notified that he had terminal cancer and would not live six months.

He took it so bravely, and didn't reveal his secret to the others, not wanting to spoil their adventure. He lasted another eight months until the day after his sixtieth birthday.

On reaching Kalgoorlie and preparing to embark on the 3000 kilometre drive home, we were notified by Val that she wouldn't be sharing the return trip as she had purchased a ticket on the bus for half the price. We never saw her again. That must have been her plan all along. But it pleased us no end, we were happy to pay the extra to get rid of her. We also had a great trip home.

RIP, George.

Double Trouble

Before biting the bullet and making the big shift to relocate to a peaceful country property west of Castlemaine, we resided in the south-east Melbourne suburb of Edithvale. The shift came naturally, as most, if not all spare moments, weekends, holidays, even the odd sickie, would see us on the road before dawn with anticipation as to what new adventure was in store. We thought, what a waste of time it was living in the big smoke when we spent our happiest times in the bush – no yapping dogs, no lawnmowers, screeching tyres, noisy neighbours, pollution, traffic lights, the list was long and made the good/bad seesaw very unbalanced.

Sure, it had its advantages. Snapper fishing in Port Phillip Bay, gummies and whiting in Westernport would be sadly missed. But all the larger provincial towns provided just about everything you could desire, including theatres, hospitals, and no waiting around on golf courses. In most districts, the larger towns can be accessed by less than half an hour's travel, and not one set of lights. Who could want more?

Before the move, one escape that provided reasonably easy access when not a lot of time was available for travel, was Tarago Reservoir. Situated only around 70 kilometres east of Dandenong, it was a comfortably easy drive. One could be on the spot and even have a trout in the bag before two hours had elapsed. Tarago is a beautiful little catchment and is the domestic water supply to the Mornington Peninsula.

Access was denied to fishermen in 1977, mainly due to the blatant disregard of a few who buggered the enjoyment of the many. Despite signage and warnings, the littering with cans, plastic bags and other rubbish continued until authorities had no option but to close the place down. After all, it was a domestic water supply. Another example of the few ignorant rednecks stuffing it up for the rest of us. Sound familiar, gun owners?

Tarago was alive with deadly tiger snakes. It was not uncommon to spot half a dozen during a day's fishing. Naturally there was no boating so shore-based anglers either floated a mudeye, sat with bait or cast lures. The adventurous could reach numerous good spots by clambering over rocky shorelines and negotiating steep drop offs, to discover lovely little hidden bays and craggy points. One tranquil morning found me traversing such terrain.

I'd already landed a nice three-pound rainbow which I'd stashed in a cool rock grotto being careful to protect it with lashings of fresh lush grass. I'd pick it up on my return. The point ahead that jutted out into the lake looked a likely spot to cast a spinner as the walls beside it were steep and narrow. Natural ledges ran along the rock wall only six to eight inches wide and a lower one of these I selected to gain access to the point. Carefully picking my way along the ledge, things were made a little easier by the fact that the next ledge up was at shoulder height. So, with rod in my left hand, I was able to balance with the right by gripping the ledge above.

Half way across my attention was taken by trout movement in the lake to my left.

As this was no place to cast or land a trout I searched ahead and there, twenty yards away, the face widened giving me access to a nice flat rock at water's edge! I continued edging forward. The plop of a surface feeder taking an insect gained my attention for another five metres, but then a sense of something near my hand on the top ledge, I slowly moved my eyes to the right making sure head movement was kept to a minimum, and there, inches from my hand was a huge tiger snake sunning himself on the narrow ledge, his beady eyes watching every move I made. My face was above the ledge just about level with his eyes, the tongue flicked. Gently and slowly I removed my hand and lowered myself to all fours and cautiously continued the journey, now underneath and hopefully out of danger. On reaching what I considered a safe distance, I slowly regained my feet and quietly stuck my head above the ledge to see where the danger lay.

"Bugger." It lay right beside me. The snake, when he first saw me, must have also decided to make good his escape by crawling (or is that slithering) in the same direction as me, only one level higher up on the ledge. He must have been as shocked as I was to find that the rude intruder was beside him again.

Down I went again, this time to the water's edge and along to where I considered it must be safe. I cautiously poked my head up and scaled the steep incline to the ledge where, with eyes darting left, right, above, and below I, gained no further sight of my reluctant companion. Finally achieving my destination at the

rocky point, I tried a dozen casts with no result.

Beyond the steep rocks, the terrain graduated down to lush rolling grass that terminated to a gravelly flat area beside the lake. Stepping down from the rocks to the flat was easy and trout movement thirty yards out enticed me into continuing my casting across the shallower waters.

I wasn't sure if it was the same tiger snake or another but a movement to my right caught my attention. This time it was fair dinkum. It meant business. It faced me and assumed the strike position, like a cobra.

It lunged forward, its head landing on the ground between my legs. I had no idea that I could achieve the splits in such a lightning move. The quick step backward, which then found me standing up to my ankles in freezing water, would have done "Dancing with the Stars" proud. Finally, I'd decided enough was enough, it was him or me, and I was holding a weapon, my trout rod.

I proceeded to whip the enraged reptile until I came to the realisation that antagonizing a snake with a trout rod does nothing but piss it off even more, and it was certainly that. But

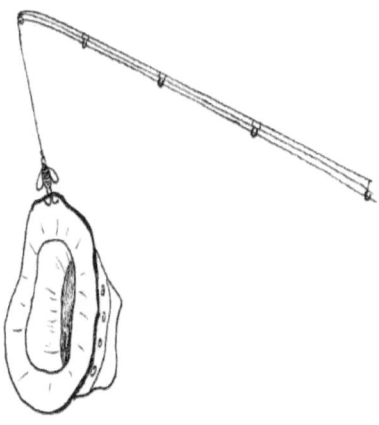

then a strange thing occurred. With rod flailing up and down, a movement above my head caught my eye. "What the?" Was I being attacked by a hawk as well? I ducked in anticipation of being struck by sharp talons. I stopped to refocus on the new danger, to discover that my floppy green hat was dangling from the end of my spinner. I'd hooked it from my own head. "Take stock, you idiot, do you realize the consequences? What if I'd hooked an eye, or worse, hooked the snake back towards me?"

He finally escaped down a rabbit hole. And I escaped embarrassment ... until now.

Maritime Cover-up

This story was shared with me by an old workmate who served on the HMAS Kanimbla during the Second World War. I'll relate a surprise connection at the end of this yarn that only revealed itself after some research.

The Kanimbla started life as a passenger liner between Cairns and Fremantle. At the outbreak of WWII, she was requisitioned and converted into an armed merchant cruiser in 1939. Now, as the HMS Kanimbla, she patrolled off the Chinese and Japanese coasts intercepting vessels that might contain suspicious cargo or contraband. In 1940 she was sent to Singapore and began patrols and escort duties. In 1941 she led a flotilla of mixed craft in a surprise attack on the Iranian Port of Bandar Shahpur. Using 300 Indian troops they captured eight German and Italian merchant vessels, two Iranian gunboats and a floating dock. During the attack she exchanged gunfire with a train, of all things, and survived repeated air attacks.

In 1943 the HMS Kanimbla was recommissioned to the HMAS Kanimbla Landing Ship Infantry. She had a compliment of 345, and the ability to transport 1280 troops.

She saw action in the Western Pacific, the South China Sea, the Philippines, Borneo and New Guinea. Also in Sydney Harbour, firing on midget subs. Her job was to conduct amphibious landings of Australian and American troops to various theatres of war around the Pacific. She was even present and contributed to the final amphibious landing of the Pacific war, landing 1267 troops at Balikpapan, Western Borneo. They witnessed and participated in bombardments, kamikaze attacks, dive bombers and the ever present threat from torpedoes and mines.

It was mid-1944 and the Pacific war was well under way. The H.M.A.S. Kanimbla was returning from the Philippines to the Islands of Halmahera and Moratai to the north of Australia, on the western end of New Guinea. My old work mate Curly, then a young able seaman, had been requisitioned to go under the scalpel of the ship's surgeon, for health reasons, in fact, a circumcision.

The operation was successfully accomplished en route, after which, the doctor advised Curl to retire early and, on awakening, to install a condom over the tender and red raw appendage prior to taking his morning shower, for protection against infection and burns.

The following morning saw the Kanimbla off Moratai. Outside, mountainous cones spewed forth an immense column of steam and smoke from the active volcano behind the township, the entire panorama tinted red by the sun's early rays made an impressive spectacle for all lucky enough to bear witness to it. Inside, Curly had donned his condom and, amid the steam and condensation of the shower, was rather less of a spectacle.

Carefully, he patted himself down, and removed his protection.

"What am I gonna do with this?" he pondered, gazing round the cubicle for some means of disposal. His eyes locked on the porthole. "Yes, that's it." He reached forward and hurled the used sheath into the Pacific Ocean. Unbeknown to Curl, the HMAS Kanimbla had docked during the night. The captain was in the process of having a group of local officials including the lord mayor and dignitaries, accompanied by a party of nurses, piped on board. They were halfway up the gangplank when the offending condom landed with a splat at their feet. The only people amused at such an affront were the sailors who witnessed the event. Although one or two nurses were observed trying to hide a smirk.

When Curl fronted the officer in charge he explained that he was only following doctor's orders and no one had told him the Kanimbla was docking. He was reprimanded for littering, but not punished.

He was overheard to mumble, "Condoms weren't always safe for seamen."

[Authors note:
The surprise connection I mentioned earlier. Remember the final amphibious landing of the Pacific war? When the Kanimbla landed 1267 troops at Balikpapan Western Borneo. Curly participated in that, and so did Lenny Ross, of an earlier story. I wonder if they ever crossed paths. I'll never know as they have both since passed on, two classy men, and I was lucky enough to meet and befriend both.]

Gotcha

Old Bob was an adventurer to the end and, despite being only months from becoming an octogenarian, he still ventured into the vast and wild Western Australian goldfields with the rest of the expedition, making up the thirteenth member to participate in the proposed twelve week prospecting trip.

Being the odd one out he drove the entire journey of around 6500 kilometres nearly on his lonesome. Members were still there to assist should he require help, so lifting heavy fuel and water containers, fixing punctures and erecting his sleeping quarters was no problem.

I said "nearly" on his lonesome. Passengers from some vehicles took turns in rotating into Bob's car for conversational reasons (mainly to keep him awake) and, on occasion, he even let them drive his pride and joy, the old Holden station wagon for short stints, the other five vehicles being 4WDs.

Apart from that, he was completely self-sufficient, preparing his own meals, washing clothes, and sharing camp duties, which he accomplished admirably and was a pleasure to camp with.

Prospecting with his heavy Deepseeker was a little more difficult for him, limiting the search area he covered. However, being so slow meant he was able to cover ground more thoroughly, and the resulting nugget finds excused his tardiness. Younger prospectors, seeing the prospective quartz ground further out, walked over nuggets in their anticipation to be the first to cover new ground. Not Bob, slow and steady.

During one early morning breakfast, camped at a place known as "Bummers Creek" (no water at all, by the way), eggs and bacon sizzling on the campfire, smoke wafting straight up into an azure sky, with shadows shortening as the sun rose, the familiar crunch of footsteps on the quartz covered ground as members rose and congregated round the communal fireplace, someone remarked, "where's old Bob?" "Haven't seen him," I replied, "is he still in his tent?' The tent was checked, "No sign of him. He's gone, we'd better find him."

We were concerned, as bob had a weak ticker, and was deaf as a post. He also had the habit of releasing huge sighs at inopportune moments that made the witness think he was about to collapse or have a heart attack. He did it once at a club meeting, during a speech from a guest speaker, to much amusement. The speaker must have thought Bob was bored shitless, but the fact was he couldn't hear himself sigh. On another occasion he was discovered lying flat out prone on the ground. The startled finder knelt and shook Bob with concern only to see his eyes flicker open with the news, "just taking a spell, mate". We were always concerned and aware that he may be too frail to continue the expedition, so we kept a keen eye on his whereabouts.

Just as a search party was being prepared, out of the scrub shuffled Bob, puffing and beaming, a huge smile on his face. "Jesus, Bob. Are you okay? We were worried sick about you". He explained, "I woke up at dawn with the first erection I've had for years, so I thought I'd celebrate by walking to the top of that hill." He pointed east to a large breakaway hill covered in quartz, some 200 metres away. Men and women roared with laughter, their relief obvious.

He had a devilish sense of humour. One of his campfire stories told of an apprentice he employed in his engineering factory in Port Melbourne. The lad was always butting into conversations when not invited. He knew the boy was listening as he related his recent fishing adventure to the foreman, "You know," he started, "two weeks ago I was fishing off Williamstown when I hooked into a nice flathead. As I reached over the side of the bloody boat my beautiful gold watch got caught on a rollick and disappeared into the drink." The Apprentice, ears pricked up, was caught on every word. He continued, "Well bugger me, this weekend we went out to the same mark and landed a couple of really nice flathead when I got hooked up with a beautiful fish, we even needed the net to land it. It was a beauty. Well, you wouldn't believe it, guess what was inside when I gutted it?" The lad couldn't contain himself any longer. With his eyes wide open with anticipation, his left finger pointed skyward, "The watch," he blurted, "the watch." Old Bob turned and replied, "Don't be bloody stupid, it was full of guts, now get back to work and mind your own business."

He amused himself no end with that one.

Straggling along behind a prospecting group that had spread out from camp in search of new ground one afternoon, members turned to a sound like a freight train roaring up the slope behind just in time to witness a large willy-willy envelope bob as it careered its way up the hill. Saltbush, gravel, stones spinifex and branches whirled and spun in the air, along with Bob's hat, disappearing into the reddened sky never to be seen again. As the mini cyclone departed its destructive course, Bob reappeared frozen to the spot like a terracotta statue, dusty but unharmed.

He continued the entire trip to return home safely with a pocket full of nuggets and another item on his bucket list fulfilled.

Wrecked 'em

When you reach a certain age it's a good idea to be checked out regularly for bowel cancer. That's what my doctor reckons anyway. Personally, I wasn't fond of the idea but could see the common sense in having the procedure done all the same. Having a camera shoved up your back passage isn't high on my things-to-do list, but with a family history of polyps and the recorded statistics of men in their fifties and later being most liable to develop cancerous growths, it was an unpleasant task best got done and over with. Come to think of it the actual colonoscopy wasn't unpleasant at all.

The nurses are gentle and reassuring and the doctors skilful and professional. It's the before, and in this case, the after, that I found most unpleasant and embarrassing. The before, in all cases, as it was in mine, is the purging of all stomach contents prior to the procedure. A large dose of bowel preparation is swallowed which turns your stomach into a concrete truck with the chute open. This in turn converts your rectum into a spray gun with no trigger control. After this the patient is obliged to starve himself until the colonoscopy is completed.

The after, in my case, was post-operative unpleasantness. Well, more embarrassment at the time, but on looking back and reliving the experience, it has had me in fits of laughter.

The morning of the big day saw me present myself to the large country hospital by nine. All the appropriate forms were signed and I was fitted out in one of those backward opening gowns and a plastic bracelet attached to my arm, after which I was ushered into a waiting cubicle. Here, the anaesthetist and doctor introduced themselves and explained the coming procedure.

After being put to sleep my stomach was to be pumped full of air, this would enable the colon camera to be inserted. He reassured me it was tiny and nothing at all like the one Channel Nine uses for the tennis. Attached to the same instrument were the means to remove any polyps encountered. They advised that a small amount of air would be introduced into the rectum to expand the colon which would allow the physician to inspect the colon walls. In my case it was enough to inflate the tyres of a grey Fergy. Did they secure me with straps to hold me down? My last memory before dropping off was being laid to one side and the angelic face of the assisting nurse smiling and assuring me with "see you when it's all ovvve…" I floated away to dreamland.

"Wake up Mr C … you're all done … can you hear me? Mr C … ?" My imaginary fishing trip to the barrier reef was interrupted by a mermaid whispering in my left ear. My eyes fluttered open. The surgeon and anaesthetist were gone. Probably on the fifth hole by now, I pondered. "You'll feel drowsy for some time and will experience stomach cramps and gas. We'll roll your bed into recovery next door and when you feel up to it, just get out of bed, walk across to the change room and dress. After that there'll be a nice sandwich and a cuppa ready for you".

They pushed my bed into the next room, which boasted a floor to ceiling sliding curtain on a railing, already prepared. Once inside, the entry curtain was slid closed for privacy.

All was quiet as I lay there semi-dozing, lapsing in and out of consciousness, the pain in my stomach was building up to a crescendo as my awareness drained back. "If I don't relieve the pain shortly, I'll explode," I thought. Drawing my legs up to my chest, finally achieved the desired result, releasing air from my stomach in an enormous expulsion of gas that would have re-

inflated the Hindenburg. It continued for what seemed like an eternity, gradually tapering off to the feeble flappings of a spent party balloon. "Thank God for that," I expressed my gratitude at the instant relief. The pain had subsided to a bearable degree. My ears pricked up as I became aware of strange sounds emanating from the other side of the curtains. I could hear shushing. And muffled giggles, the shushing again.

Quietly slipping out of bed, I cautiously parted the curtain to one side to reveal that my recovery room was in fact the west end of the waiting room and there, a mother was having no success at all in containing the amusement of her 12-year-old son.

Seated around the room on an obviously donated lounge setting were four more adults all with huge smirks on their faces. My eyes darted in search of the change room door, my escape route.

And there it was some 4 metres across the floor. "Could I make it across the open ground without being observed?" Quietly, I shuffled across the room, and damn near made it when the small boy chuckled out loud. I glanced back to discover that he was pointing at me, or moreover my open gown at the rear which was displaying my bare butt in plain view. While dressing, the nurse popped her head in and relayed the news that my sandwich and cuppa were ready.

"Give us a call when you're dressed. Come this way," she directed, "we've set up a trolley for you." I tagged along behind her, down the corridor, two left turns and through a large half glass door lined with stainless steel.

Inside were my goodies, all set up at a lounge chair, a woman and her 12-year-old son and four other adults. Due to renovations at the hospital, this one rather large room was serving as both waiting and recovery rooms. It was extremely difficult in making eye contact, what with the little smart-arse making muffled fart noises to his great amusement. Mum was still nudging and shushing, to no avail. Scoffing the sandwich, I washed it down with the cuppa and prepared to escape the continued embarrassment. I could feel the deep grumblings of another stomach contraction as I approached the exit door, which released just in time for me to leave my captive audience with a parting salvo.

Their laughter resounding down the corridor as I departed the hospital was reward enough.

Lost and Found

It was the early eighties and a successful prospecting trip to the Victorian goldfields saw a small group of mates detecting the "Potato" diggings near Kingower, so named because of the abundance of heavy gold. Prospectors of the time were reported to toss each shovel full of paydirt into the air and catch it on the blade. If a clunk was heard the sod was investigated further.

The trip was "successful", not only because of the unearthing of four small nuggets, the largest weighing in at five pennyweights detected in some shallow diggings.

But ranging further up a slight rise which overlooked a thousand shallow holes, I received a target under a gnarled old tree in virgin ground. Kicking the twigs and leaves to one side revealed a glint of gold. It was a ring.

It wasn't just any ring. It was a beautifully hand crafted gold wedding ring, designed with wavy scallops on both sides; fashioned we guessed by a bush jeweller using local gold.

We could only surmise. Was the digger's camp located under that old tree? Was the woman watching her loved ones toiling in the field below, dreaming of untold riches?

Who knows. She must have been devastated with her loss. But my wife Faye was delighted to receive it when I presented it to her on my return, and wore it daily from that day onwards. Well, most of the time.

The find convinced her that detecting was a good thing because, with her interest fired up and a new Minelab, she became a keen prospector. And a good one.

1989 saw us camped 3000 kilometres away in a hidden valley

south-east of Leonora, Western Australia, just south of a range of dividing hills.

The new site had been located a few days earlier when my son Dave and I had reconnoitred the area from our previous camp, in search of sites with potential to prospect. Some thirty kilometres north we found our way through low-lying scrub, five creek crossings and flats dense with undergrowth, to break through into a series of quartzy hills rising to the dividing range. The area looked great with quartz covered slopes and hills everywhere. Yet, the early prospectors mustn't have thought so, as there seemed no evidence of their testing the ground. No diggings, dry-blowings, costeans or test holes anywhere, yet the spot looked great to us. The only evidence of previous visitors was hundreds of tree stumps cut clean just above ground level in some of the flatter valleys. Probably used for shoring up mineshafts in the nearby goldfields some twenty kilometres away; or firewood.

Half an hour's detecting and Dave called from a rise a hundred metres to my right, "Got one," he jubilantly announced, and sure enough, a quarter ounce of beautiful gold, dripping with spittle, was presented on the palm of his hand. He'd cleaned it in his mouth.

We scanned the surrounding slopes and hills with gold-crazed eyes. "The potential of this place is amazing, we have to relocate camp immediately," I stated. We couldn't return to relay the new find quick enough. After breaking camp and restocking with provisions we made our way back to the new site.

"Let's not camp right on the spot for fear of alerting any passers-by to the fact that a party is camped in the middle of nowhere, for what reason. Let's find a camp that's hidden away and return on foot to prospect," I offered, and this we did, finding a great little site under trees at the end of a dead-end hidden valley, well off the track, perfect.

Now, with our new camp well set up, each morning would see us march diagonally over the series of hills that now separated us from the original find, probably two kilometres north-west, where only another two small pieces turned up.

But the ground falling away from camp was a flattish, gently sloping valley floor about 200 metres wide and proved very productive. The ground was covered in quartz which dropped into "crabholes", a local description of soft powdery depressions spread across the valley floor which the quartz seemed to disappear into. The larger nuggets, up to 3 ounces, were located in these at varying depths, and the surrounding flat virgin ground produced many small pieces, with the odd specimen in quartz up to the size of an apricot.

Night prospecting by the light of the moon was exhilarating, no flies, no mosquitoes, no hot sun or wind, (the wind always died at evening) and the operator could concentrate and discriminate the slightest alteration in the detector's hum. It was magical and exciting.

One had to keep an eye out for camels and goats and, worse still, the odd death adder, but a book could be read by the moonlight, so there were no worries really.

Three weeks had passed when an Aboriginal stockman named Cyril arrive over the crest of a hill on a motorbike. He introduced himself and enquired as to how long we've been here as he's never seen anyone in this paddock before.

"This paddock? I haven't even seen a fence, how big is this paddock?" I asked. "Forty thousand acres," he replied matter of factly.

One paddock, forty thousand acres, made our forty acres back home look like a tennis court.

Every few weeks, Cyril would drop in for a cuppa and a chat. He even brought his wife along on one trip. It seemed he'd been quite an athlete in his youth winning the 100 metre final in the World Junior Olympics in, I think he said, Singapore. But buggered his promising athletics career by running a chain saw through his thigh. That'll do it.

Supplementing our diet with local fare, he remarked one evening on a rabbit we'd strung up between a couple of knotty old sandalwood trees.

"Like underground mutton, I see," said Cyril. "Got a rifle have ya?" "Yes, mate," I replied, "We broke the pipes on the van's refrigerator coming through all those creek crossings and have no means of keeping meat fresh for more than a week, (thank God for Long Life milk), so until our next trip for provisions we've learned how to cook rabbit in a dozen different ways."

"What about goat?" he questioned. "Tried that."

"No mate, we've heard the pastoralists frown on visitors knocking off their wild goats, so we've left them alone."

"Yeah, Brudda, that's right, but if I give you permission and I herd a mob of goats in for you it's okay." I was chuffed to hear him refer to me as Brudda, I was one of the family.

So the next morning, with arrangements made, I set up with the rifle at the nearest well 3 kilometres away. Nine o'clock was the designated time, and about 10 minutes past I could hear in the distance the motorbike purring, then revving, changing gears, louder, roaring, until over the quartz ridge a mob of about thirty wild goats loomed into view, running at full tilt.

"The little white one," yelled Cyril, "drop him now." The poor little bugger had hardly time to become a goat teenager, but, as ordered, the kill was swift and sudden. Just behind the front shoulder.

"Good shot," complimented Cyril, "now we'll prepare him."

He expertly strung the goat on the windmill frame and prepared the beast for the table, removing front and hind quarters after skinning and gutting. "Here", he said, "you take this," handing me a large hind leg, "I'll take the rest back to the station."

The leg was slow-roasted in the camp oven, smeared with olive oil, herbs, and lamb spices, along with spuds, onions and carrots and turned out beautiful and succulent; unlike the next meal Cyril provided.

Another week had passed and the distant familiar sound of a motorbike broke the everlasting silence. He arrived in camp in a cloud of dust, with a large goanna draped across the handlebars.

Letting it slide to the ground he announced, Try this, mate. Good tucka." And off he zoomed.

Our eyes met, "What in hell are we gonna do with this? And "I'm not touching that thing," from Faye.

We skinned it, gutted it, wrapped the choice pieces in aluminium foil after rolling them in a mixture of flour, paprika, garlic, and herbs, and cooked it on a grid over the fire.

It turned out like old army boots, tough as old leather.

When asked of our culinary experience next visit by Cyril, we described the preparation given to the hapless reptile and the result. He admonished us with, "Christ, you don't need all that bullshit, just chuck it on the fire whole, turning occasionally, it cooks in its own skin, you bloody amateurs are hopeless."

We all laughed at our misguided efforts.

And so we come full circle, back to the ring which started this long winded reminiscence.

On prospecting ventures, Faye had a habit of removing the ring from her finger and placing it on the ground to tune her detector to the present conditions and reassure herself that it was functioning correctly. Twice we had to return to areas that she had chained, and twice we recovered the lost ring. (Chaining involves dragging a length of chain behind you tied to your belt with a stout cord. This creates a line on the ground indicating where you've been, good for covering an area thoroughly.)

The third time it disappeared for good, it was nowhere to be found and she was beside herself with concern and self-doubt.

We had all been travelling up to a kilometre away from camp in search of gold, and one morning as we returned prior to lunch she met us with, " How'd you go boys?" All we could reply was with open hands, "No nothing, seems like we've cleaned up".

"Put your hand out," she ordered. "What do you think of these?" Into my hand she dumped half a dozen beautiful slugs of gold weighing close to an ounce, and a small half ounce specimen.

"What the, where the, how the?" We were gobsmacked.

She explained, "When you lot took off early I thought I'd do the washing and hang it up. As I had no idea where you were I decided I'd detect around camp till you arrived back for lunch. We've camped right on a patch. Look," she pointed out a scratching near the van's wheel. "I even found one there."

Lunch was completed very quickly that day and many nuggets and specimens turned up over the following days, some nearly two ounces in weight. Some were found beside the stumps left by woodcutters, which really amazed me, as some nuggets were in plain view on the surface. I suppose woodcutters weren't looking for gold.

I found myself drawn towards the clothesline and a third sweep of the machine produced a target which turned out to be a beautiful specimen with 2.5 ounces of gold, the size of half an apple. It was in plain view right on the surface, we must have walked on it to hang the washing up. But then I found another target right under a pair of pants hanging on the line, I looked down and there it was ... the ring, home again, shining like a long lost friend.

We concluded that it wasn't really lost at all, but secreted away in the cuff of Faye's pants and dislodged when they were hung up.

She was absolutely rapt and has never misplaced it since, still wearing it to this day.

The Long Drop

After three long hot months prospecting on the dry Western Australian goldfields some 400 kilometres north of Kalgoorlie, we yearned for the sound of surf pounding on golden beaches. You don't realize just how much red dust, constant quartz underfoot, no rivers or lakes, and drinking and washing in bore water makes you yearn for the glisten of sunlight through curling breakers, and the fresh, sweet smell of salt air. Don't get me wrong, there's nothing like being camped in the remote and secluded outback, and there's especially nothing wrong with finding the odd patch of nuggets. What a rush. Just you, nature and the elements, how good is that?

But for those raised in Victoria, where some kind of water experience is nearly a daily event, be it lake, river or sea, then the old ticker starts pumping even harder at the (excuse the pun) prospect.

Seventy kilometres east of the beautiful Western Australian town of Esperance saw us camped not 100 metres from such surf.

Locals had given us directions to this remote location between two national parks. As we had a dog, our party was not permitted in the park. This suited us down to the ground, as none of the party considered camping in regulated national parks with a hundred tourists camping.

With the assistance of a snatch strap, and deflating the tyres, both vehicles with vans attached were able to negotiate the soft sand dunes that guarded the approach to this little oasis, with the vehicle ahead assisting its mate behind and, after traversing something like 17 kilometres, we breached the last dune.

There, below us, the track changed from sand to firm brown soil, the terrain to coastal scrub and greenery, and our first whiff of the sea. The track snaked its way through a canopy of massive banksia trees, the largest we'd ever seen, all in bloom, and terminated beside an old timber and corrugated iron whaler's hut, nestled at the base of a low sand dune. Fresh water was laid on, as the tank beside the hut was still intact, despite the years, and full to the brim. The site afforded an ideal windbreak and shade cover. What a fantastic spot, those old whalers knew their stuff.

We scaled the low dune and before us to the left, the coastline stretched towards the Great Australian Bight, as far as the eye could see, fringed with coastal scrub and banksias, breakers crashing on the sand. To the right the surf finished against a red rocky outcrop of land which reached a good kilometre out into the sea, a perfect little bay for the original settlers to launch and retrieve their clinker built whale boats. We had it to ourselves, there wasn't a soul to be seen for miles, and we knew that access was only available via our track or, many kilometres away, at the national parks. Out to sea, a number of small islands would have given refuge to those whalers that weren't able to make it back to camp during rough weather. The beautiful blue-green sea reached south to the horizon, nothing but seawater between us and Antarctica.

After the desert, this place was heaven. And so was the fishing. If the surf was too rough, we could walk out on the rocky ledge and fish safely into the swell. Clear patches of sandy bottom could be seen between the darker weed beds, and casting into these one could witness the dark shapes of large fish as they entered from the weed beds, to snatch the bait and take off.

By Victorian standards the salmon fishing was magnificent. One

Author Geoff, Ritchie and son David

morning, in just two hours, we landed seventeen salmon, all over nine pound. The fish we needed for food we kept in deep rock pools that the ages had carved out of the bedrock and were located all along the outcrop.

And so it was, settled into this wonderful campsite under the protection of the huge banksias and below the leeside of the last dune, we were sung to sleep by the repetitious sloshing of the distant waves.

Early the next morning, keen as mustard, I rigged the surf rod I'd mollycoddled for the whole trip, and with anticipation high, trundled over the ridge of sand dunes in front of camp, breaking the thin hard crust that an overnight shower had formed on the surface. The two women, Faye and Sheryl, mate Ritchie and son Dave were still in dreamland, oblivious to the beautiful tranquil morning. Only the occasional gull broke the silence as I trudged along, even the surf was becalmed, just the odd lazy wave finding its way to the shore and collapsing on the sand as though it just couldn't be bothered causing a fuss. The coastline was mine alone for as far as the eye could see. It was magical.

Selecting a suitable gutter was easy as the ridge of dunes commanded a wonderful view of the surf and the dark blue-green deeper gutters were obvious. So, with anticipation, about a kilometre east of camp, I eased my way down the dune to set up in front of an obvious gutter about 60 metres out, baited up and cast the ganged hook rig out over the darker coloured channel to the far side. I reeled in till the bait started to drop into the deep, lay back on the sand with my head propped up on one arm, and admired the view. Wow, this was so idyllic.

A large crab, a bunch of seaweed, and two nice salmon later, I happened to glance back toward camp, and through the distant haze a solitary figure appeared. Ten minutes passed and the figure, which was walking in an awkward swagger, not unlike Charlie

Chaplin, came into view. It was Dave. When questioned on his unusual manner of movement, the reason became understandable. It seems that not far from camp, on his early morning walk, he had discovered an old long drop thunder box.

This old outhouse type toilet must have been constructed by the whalers and was still in pretty good order. Not being one to miss an opportunity, Dave thought he'd make use of the first real sit down toilet he'd seen in months. Sure beats crouching behind a bush. Lifting the lid, he made himself comfortable and was admiring the banksias through the door when a searing pain shot through his loins, then another, and another.

In agony he burst through the door, his pants around his ankles, a swarm of angry bees in hot pursuit. The moon had appeared early for them, that morning.

He escaped, but his private parts didn't, and as he wasn't going to permit anyone else at camp to attend his medical needs, he carried out his own repairs. Not that they would have anyway.

Thing a Thong of Thickness

It was one of those crystal clear, calm mornings you only get in the outback Western Australian goldfields. The camp fire smoke spiralled almost perfectly vertically and dissipated into the rich dawning blueness. A single line of five wild goats following a well-worn ribbon of a track returned from their morning pilgrimage to the well, some miles to the west. Undulating slopes of heavy quartz stretched to the distant ranges north of base camp. Interspersed with spindly sandalwood trees, the beautiful salmon gum and quondong trees, fringed with patches of spinifex and low, stunted desert foliage, the place was like a scene on an alien planet.

Recent rain had excited the growth of millions of ground cover daisies and, wherever one looked, the shock of a new carpet of colour reached to the horizon. Mixed with the pink trunk and glossy green leaves of the salmon gum and the red earth, all topped off with the bright blue sky, it was like living in an Albert Namitjira landscape painting, except the intoxicating fragrance gave it all away.

The terrain was absolute murder on footwear and a good pair of boots didn't last long on the uncompromising quartz. Prospecting the quartzy flats and slopes day after day resembled crunching eternally on a bed of rice bubbles. Ritchie had destroyed his boots over the previous weeks and the only footwear that remained were a pair of thongs (flip-flops), until our next trip for provisions some hundred miles away. So it was with these he marched off into the hills for his morning's detecting.

The previous evening's coals only required a few dry twigs for it to reignite. The bacon was sizzling merrily when off to the side, the familiar crunch of gravel met my ears. But this was different. Instead of an even crunch, crunch, came an unfamiliar crunch, pause, crunch, pause. I looked up to see a most unusual sight. Ritchie was returning early, decidedly favouring one foot, the other being used on tippy toe. He was also missing the shirt sleeve of one arm. Now there's nothing worse than being caught short in the bush with no paper, hence the missing shirt sleeve; but the foot. Had he sprained an ankle? Been snake bitten?

"What happened mate?" I inquired. "Are you okay?" His reply not only put me off breakfast, but had my uncontrollable laughter wake up the rest of the camp.

He'd managed to find his way to a small rise some two kilometres away that had been productive the previous day, producing half a dozen nice little nuggets all under three pennyweights. After only fifteen minutes prospecting an uncontrollable call of nature had him stamping his feet in anticipation and looking for a suitable site to carry out his morning movement in comfort.

All in camp, when venturing beyond eyeshot, carry with them in a small survival shoulder bag a few essentials, which includes a water or drink bottle, matches, small compass, some nibbles like barley sugar or Lifesavers and a small roll of toilet paper.

His evacuation was a huge relief, but that's when the good news finished. He searched the survival bag. "Bugger, no toilet paper." After ripping and using the sleeve off his flannelette shirt he stood up to pull his shorts back into position.

Unbeknown to Ritchie, the recently departed had toppled over like the leaning tower of Pisa, and lay steaming across the heel of his left thong. Naturally, as he squatted, the thong was flat, his heel raised, but as he rose to the vertical position his heel lowered down onto the offending hard hit. Subsequently, his foot shot out of the thong, like a rabbit with a ferret in hot pursuit, as he stumbled forwards trying to regain his balance.

It was obvious that the terrain was absolutely unnavigable in bare feet and the only water for miles was back at camp. He cleaned it as best he could and hobbled back to camp experiencing the most uncomfortable walk in his life.

His next trip for provisions, and new boots, was brought forward to the next morning immediately. This wasn't ever happening again.

Summer Love

Jenny Schiffer was a doll, a living doll, a goddess. She was so sweet, so innocent. Her angelic face had a presence about it that commanded attention to the point of distraction. She didn't walk, she flowed wherever she went, and her perfume was intoxicating. It wasn't a smell it was a fragrance that was hers alone, and it lingered long after she had gone. I knew she'd been through the corridor ten minutes after the event. I fancied she had some German heritage in her blood, her honey coloured tresses which caressed and framed her full, slightly squarish jawline, hung down to her shoulders. Her deep azure-blue eyes, complemented by her smooth blemish-free olive skin, were just plain mesmerizing, as I had discovered on the few occasions that we had spoken. I had forced myself to look away for fear of being drawn into those hypnotic pools of electric blue.

She stood tall and proud and moved with the confidence of an elite athlete, a reflection of her standing in her favourite pursuit, women's hockey. My heart would race at the prospect of a smile, and a word from those full perfect lips was expectant bliss. A chance meeting was something to fantasize and dream about all morning. What would be my chances if I played my cards right? Would it be remotely possible for Jenny to actually consider a date? I was seventeen, and did I have the hots for Jenny Schiffer.

The summer holidays were approaching fast, we had already experienced a couple of those hot, still mornings that the local cicadas had borne testament to; their monotonous and deafening blare had already raised the voices of conversations in city and suburb alike.

Her office was on the ground floor of the huge government office complex in central Melbourne, and every opportunity I had to detour through her domain would be accepted with expectant optimism. As I was the youngest male in the office, and strong enough to handle the multitude of orders, as well as local dogsbody and gopher, it was my duty to make the morning pilgrimage from the eighth floor to the street side sandwich shop and café, where the morning tea orders would be waiting for me. The thrill of the chase always beckoned me, eternally hopeful of a glimpse of Jenny, a smile, a word.

It was on one of these trips it happened. I left the shop armed with a tray of goodies, milkshakes, coffee, tea and coke, a mixed variety of sandwiches, doughnuts and assorted snacks. And manoeuvred my way up the granite steps, through the marble arched entrance into the huge entrance foyer.

Italian tiles of a dozen different colours, displayed in dizzying patterns, echoed my footsteps as I detoured down the corridor that led past Jenny's office. And the fragrance was there, lingering. Walk slower, maybe she'll open the door before I pass. There were female voices as I drew near, and an unmistakable giggle, but no luck, maybe later.

Retracing my steps to the main entrance foyer where the elevator could be found beside the staircase. With hands full, I pressed the button with my elbow, and patiently waited while the old fashioned rattler decided to obey my command, and return to the ground floor. I watched as the clock-like dial above the door indicated its progress.

Pressing eight was even more difficult, but with practice I'd mastered the task. Holding the tray with both hands, an extended pinky did the job. On a previous occasion I'd learnt the hard way, the tray had to be kept level or the contents would slide to one side. This in turn created a new centre of balance which found me trying to compensate by raising one hand which turned the whole shooting match into a freaking conveyor belt, all over me. It was an empty lift and as there were no other lights glowing on the button console I knew that I would express right to my floor. It's funny, when you think back, that things don't always seem to go as one plans.

Who knows, it might have been the All-Bran I had for breakfast, or the egg and lettuce roll I'd scoffed down at the coffee shop, but all of a sudden an overwhelming urge to break wind came over me. Hey, I was in an empty elevator, go for it son, and let it rip. I did.

It would have got me first prize in the boy's locker room, and was it on the nostrils. Old Squizzy's sulphur trick in the science lab at Prahran Tech had nothing on this. Wherever I backed to in the lift it followed like an Exocet missile. It hung like the aftermath of a nuclear explosion, an invisible wall that forced its victim to gasp and reel back.

Well pleased with my effort, I was having a private chuckle to myself when, horror of horrors, the fifth floor light flickered on and the elevator began to slow. With a ding, the lift stopped, the door opened and there standing in all her glory, was … Jenny Schiffer, my idol.

The girl of my dreams stood before me, we had an empty lift, and I'd just dropped the biggest clanger in history. She smiled enticingly, fluttering her ample eyelashes and entered the chamber of surprises. I returned her smile, and not being game enough to accept the responsibility of trapping the poor girl for the next eleven floors (three up and eight down) I departed the lift and continued my journey via the fire escape, knowing that, as the door closed on Jenny, it also closed on me.

My embarrassment was such that from that day forward I went out of my way to avoid any contact whatsoever with her. I hardly ever saw her again, but when I did she totally ignored me. I guess my presence conjured up images of stockyards or sewerage farms. I suppose the most valuable lesson I learnt out of the whole miserable saga, was never fart in a lift, unless there were others present. I also learnt to keep a straight face.

Blind Mullet

February in Melbourne can be mighty warm. After toiling all day in the hot sun laying bricks, Bazza and Vic had had enough. The new estate at Patterson Lakes, a beach side suburb of south-east Melbourne, was well under construction. The two mates, self-employed partners, usually started early in summer to beat the stifling heat and by the time 3 o'clock came around it was about as hot as it was going to get. As it was pre-daylight savings it was pretty much the peak time of day for heat and the obvious time to clean the tools and mixer and square up for the day. "Whadya reckon mate," asked Vic, "do you fancy a swim and cool off at the Edithvale beach?" "Sounds great," replied Baz, "we'll grab a pack of bitter on the way."

By the time they had arrived, the beach was starting to swell with an influx of school students, classes over for the day, which, when added to the regulars that frequented the beach, made for quite a crowd. Finding a vacant plot of sand between bathers didn't take all that long, despite that fact. They always packed swimming trunks and towels in the truck for just such occasions as an evening at the beach after a stinker was a welcome relief. It was something to anticipate and a regular occurrence in summer.

Being bricklayers, there were no inhibitions about body shape, as both were well proportioned, tanned and exhibited muscular frames to die for, a testament to the extreme workout their regular job provided. What with wheelbarrows full of concrete and mortar, hods of bricks, heavy planks and scaffold and exposure to all the elements, it was either muscle up or find another occupation. They did receive pretty good remuneration and all who witnessed what they had to do for it agreed, they earned every cent.

After a refreshing swim they trundled back up through the sand to the small clearing they'd discovered between a fat lady under a beach umbrella and a young couple entwined together oblivious to the world around them. Cracking a tinny each, they settled back to relax and admire the view. The sun was one quarter above the horizon, shimmering and glistening through the small wavelets, the sea becalmed and flat. In the distance were fishing boats dotted across the panorama, obviously trying to land some pinky snapper feeding on the scallop and mussel beds before nightfall. The familiar aromas of suntan oil and ice-cream wafted down the beach, as the screeching of gulls fighting over a hot chip tossed to them by a small boy with a cricket bat disturbed the relative peace.

"Hey Baz," Vic finally broke the silence.

"Yes, mate," replied Barry inquisitively. "I'm busting, and there's no toilet for miles." Baz thought for a moment then, "Go out in the water mate. The tide's going out, no one will know." "Great idea" said Vic, "I'm off."

He disappeared into the sea. Bazza followed his progress, winding his way through the bathers until way out, only Vic's head was visible. He smiled to himself knowingly and thought, "Jeez, he's certainly going a long way out to relieve himself." Half a tinny later, Vic reappeared and flopped down on the sand beside his mate.

"What a relief, I couldn't have lasted much longer." He resumed his acquaintance with his beer and settled back on one elbow. Then, "What's that smell?" enquired Baz. "Yeah" replied Vic, "I was gonna ask the same thing. Jeez, it's ripe." They scanned the surrounding crowd but nothing untoward revealed itself. "It's closer than you think," said Barry. "Turn around," he ordered. Vic rolled over on one side to reveal a long brown skid mark from the base of his back to his neck, sand peppering the entire length like frosting on a chocolate mud cake.

"You're kidding, I thought you only wanted to pee. How could you lay a blind mullet with all this crowd around?" Baz muttered incredulously. "What am I going to do? I can't hang around here like this," said Vic.

Bazza, enjoying his embarrassment, was having great difficulty in containing himself. "Get back in the water, and don't come back till it's gone, you're not getting in my truck stinking like Pepé Le Pew." And so, Vic, with his beach towel draped over his shoulders, re-entered the water where he scrubbed and towelled his back till it hurt. He was so thankful the tide was going out.

A Bloody Day

Dogs are my favourite animal but sheep killers in rural Victoria will not be tolerated and farmers are quite within their rights to shoot offenders on sight. During the weeks prior to lambing season in spring 1998, I was returning from an uneventful afternoon's fishing trip to a local lake, negotiating the 4WD down the gravelly track that leads to my small farmlet of forty acres.

The property, which is bordered by state forest, is mostly cleared and, being secluded and remote, is just to our liking. Solar powered with back up diesel generator and a small wind generator on a forty foot tower, all our power needs are met admirably.

All the land on the southern approach to our gate was owned by Greg, a small-time sheep farmer who supplemented his meagre truck driving income by running a small flock of sheep averaging around 200 beasts, which produced extra fine merino wool, as low as 18 microns.

His 200 acres, like ours, was mostly cleared on the lower flats and rose to undulating, heavily timbered country on the upper slopes. Two erosion gullies in the shape of a v wound their way through the property starting high on the east slopes and traversing the sheep paddocks, petering out to nothing as they eventually joined and found their way into small creeks that emptied into a huge lake to the east, the one I'd spent the day fishing in. These erosion gullies were, in places, up to 20 feet wide and 10 feet deep. A great secluded highway for foxes to patrol and get close to sheep during lambing season.

But it wasn't foxes that caught my eye this time. Slowing to a crawl as I approached our gate, something unusual attracted my attention, something different in Greg's paddock on the right.

As far as the eye could see, large patches of white were randomly spaced in the paddock off to the distant forest line. "What the?" I braked to better take in the spectacle. Sheep, as many as twenty, were lying dead and dying in random patterns off into the distance. Torn apart, their white wool strewn in irregular and bloody displays stood out like beacons on the verdant spring pasture. I couldn't believe the sight, it was as if they had plummeted from an overhead passing 747, hitting the ground like bombs, the white wool mushrooming out from each carcass up to twenty feet.

I scanned the paddock. Up against the western fence were fifty or so shivering sheep, hunkering together in frightful anticipation of their impending fate.

On the other side of the nearest erosion gully about fifty yards out was another dying sheep beside which were what I originally thought were two fire blackened stumps, which are common in the area. I looked again.

"Stumps be buggered." Lying on their bellies, two dogs, completely engrossed in their murderous adventure, were in the process of dispatching another helpless victim. One, a huge bull-mastiff, had his back to me, the other, a Rottweiler cross was

facing me but busy crunching the throat of his victim, shaking the hapless beast from side to side like a rag doll.

"What do I do?" They ignored the diesel motor as I quietly drove through the gate and wound my way up to the house. My first duty was to notify Greg's wife Mary by phone. He was still on the road so she would notify the ranger for instructions.

Ten minutes later, Ken the ranger rang me to say he would be at least half an hour and "did I have a rifle?" "Yes," I replied, "what should I do?" "Go down there, don't endanger yourself by getting too close, and fire a couple of shots in their direction to scare them away. That'll do till I get there."

Unlocking the gun cabinet, I picked up the 15 shot jw-21 Chinese made lever action fitted with a Japanese hunter scope and loaded it. Not much of a rifle, but it was accurate enough to maintain an inch group at fifty yards and was good enough for rabbits and other vermin.

I could never understand since the Howard government's introduction of the gun buy back scheme in October '96 that I had to hand in my beautiful Ruger 10 shot automatic, but I could legally purchase and use a 15 shot lever action. Had I been a nut case like the mass murderers Knight and Bryant I had 5 more shots at my disposal ... crazy.

As I'd just returned from fishing, my clothing was appropriate, subdued dull colours that wouldn't spook or alert fish... or dogs. I was ready.

Making my way down the hill I was surprised to see both animals as I had left them, mauling the now dead sheep, oblivious to the outside world.

By lining up behind large trees either side of the track, I was able to negotiate both barbed wire fences giving me access to Greg's paddock. Forty yards in front of me was the erosion gully and another fifty yards beyond, the dogs. If I could only make it undetected to the gully, I could have fired a couple of shots from the safe side of both fences. But, after considering the possible consequences, I decided these killers would only escape and live to continue their blood lust on another day, on another property. So it was now or never.

If I could make it to the gully, I could pop my head over the ledge and get a clear fifty yard shot. The last twenty yards was open ground, no cover except low grass, but, by watching the dogs' head movements, I managed to belly crawl the distance undetected and finally slide into the deep ravine. So far, so good. My heart was pounding in my throat with anticipation, not to mention apprehension.

The cracking and crunching of bones carried on the breeze as I raised my head over the quartzy ledge. Both still there. Must be tired, or full, I mused. A hell of a lot bigger than I'd guessed. Shit.

To gain purchase for a steady shot I eased my shoulders and both arms over the rim and unlocked the safety catch. The larger dog, the Rottweiler cross, had his head down facing me, oblivious to my presence. I lined up the sights at the exposed head, figuring if the shot was high it would still penetrate between the shoulder blades achieving the desired result, a fatal shot. But then, what would I know?

Steadying, I let out a three quarter breath, holding the last quarter and squeezed the trigger. As they say in the classics, "all hell broke loose."

Both dogs sprang to attention, and both took off at full pace, straight towards me. No time to think. Stand my ground and remain steady. I managed four shots as they neared. Not an easy accomplishment considering I was trying to focus through a telescopic sight with the targets looming larger than life towards me, and being left handed, had to operate the bolt by crossing my left hand over the breach.

I was now standing head, shoulders and torso above the protective ledge of the washout, in full view, and as they neared, found it impossible to focus through the sights. It was a matter of sight along the barrel and hope. Ten yards out, they turned to the right, doing a complete circle, and disappeared off up the hill into the heavy timber and out of sight.

I followed them with a few snapshots, with no apparent result. "Jesus, how could I have missed, was I shaking that much?" My heart was thumping like a stamp battery at a goldmine, and as my close up view of the killers revealed as they turned, they were both huge balls of muscle with massive heads. Blood from their killing spree stained both snouts and lower neck, even down the front of both legs.

Ten minutes later, Mary turned up with Ken the ranger and I explained the recent turn of events. "Not much of a shot mate," he drawled, with a smirk. "And, what didn't you understand about not getting too close?"

Fancying myself as a pretty fair shot I was rather appalled at my amateurish showing.

"Right," he ordered, "the three of us spread out and track up the hill, eyes down, look for signs." Five minutes elapsed, then Mary called out, "Look … here." We converged on her sighting and there among the leaf litter, a spot of blood. Redemption, I'd hit one. Further up, another, and another. We fanned out, scanning higher ground, Ken the Ranger disappeared out of sight above us. Then, through the trees, "Geoff, up here, mate." I homed in on his voice a hundred yards higher.

"I've got an apology to make to you," he stated. "Have a look at this." At his feet was the Rottweiler, dead. "Look at the collar, mate." I knelt and inspected the leather collar. A fresh furrow ran from one side to the other. Ken observed, "that first shot was dead centre, hit the collar and deflected. No wonder they took off in a hurry, you must have hit him with the chest shot as he ran past."

I was vindicated. We continued up the slope, then more blood. "Hey look! More signs you've hit both of them."

His new-found respect for my marksmanship was warming, but I hated to think the animal may be wounded and in pain, we had to locate it and dispatch it. Another two hundred yards and this time it was Mary again, "Over here."

There, straddled across the bottom wire of the corner fence line was the bull-mastiff. On closer inspection, there was a fresh hole through the tip of one ear and the fatal shot had entered behind the rear rib on the right side. I must have got them both as they were broadside, turning up to the right. He was strong enough to run three hundred yards before expiring on the fence wire.

It's a pity, because both dogs were loved pets of owners from the nearest town, three miles away.

They had perpetrated other killings on nearby properties and had developed a blood lust to kill. The owners, tracked by the collar identifications, were ordered to compensate Greg and

Mary for the loss of twenty sheep and one prized breeder ram, a considerable sum for simple neglect.

The lesson to be learnt is always know where your pets are, and no matter how sweet they are at home, primeval instinct kicks in when they are unsupervised and influenced by pack mentality. Even if the "pack" is only two. It could be expensive to all parties.

Rani

Fifteen and a half years she'd blessed our lives. Unbelievers would say, "but she's only a dog." Tell that to any family that's had the experience of being owned by a dog. Their devoted love, loyalty, and attachment, mischievousness, even humour, is unmatched by any other animal. Their ability to surprise and amuse, learn and even teach is something to behold and their aim to please, no matter what the circumstances, is beyond understanding, in spite of the way they are treated by some owners.

They say that fifteen years in doggy lingo is equivalent to over a hundred in human terms, and is a great lifetime for a Wiemeraner, but it still broke our hearts when she left us. My very first memory of her was the long drive to Ararat where the breeder lived on a small farm.

The plan was to detour overnight and stay in the bush with a group of my prospecting mates at Campbelltown, have a quick prospect on Saturday morning and then leave early enough to keep our three o'clock appointment with the breeder. A dozen of us did the usual bush camp with a roaring log fire, toasted crumpets with a coffee or ale, followed by a restless night in anticipation of what the coming day may bring.

Watching the dawn over a rekindled camp fire with the night mist still clinging to the lower contours, while the surrounding birdlife wakes up, is another of life's pleasures. After a hearty breakfast, we all set off into the field, raring to go. Two hours of swinging a detector, digging up nails and bullets can be rather tiresome, but, a hundred yards below an old mineshaft, on a long sweeping slope, my detector signalled a faint target.

This was different. It was deep, in undisturbed ground and the structure was quartzy gravel. Nine inches of overburden revealed a beautiful three quarter ounce slug of gold.

Later, I was to discover that it was the only nugget found on that trip despite a few old coins and relics, so I was chuffed to think that the day I was to purchase our new pup would deliver such a lucky find. Was it some sort of omen?

On arrival at the breeder's home we were ushered into a warm compound, carpeted with straw, where the three remaining pups of the litter were tumbling and chasing each other in blissful joy. I knelt and clucked my tongue, the two larger pups ignored my attempts at attention.

But the runt trotted over and nuzzled my open palm, unafraid and friendly.

"That'll do us," I suggested to Faye. She nodded and the deal was done.

That first year of her life brought us lots of warm cuddly memories with a number of really unpleasant ones thrown in. All dog owners suffer the embarrassing moments of teaching their pet's toilet habits and where not to perform them, like the lounge or kitchen floor.

My most unpleasant recollection (and by the way, it may have been unpleasant for me but everyone else seems to find it extraordinarily humorous) was when I'd let Rani out (yes, we named her after an Indian Princess) into the backyard to play and attend to nature's call.

The backyard, being completely enclosed, was a totally safe environment for her to roam. She could explore to her heart's content, chew and taste, smell the flowers and do all the exciting things a newborn pup experiencing life for the first time wanted to do, and in complete safety, I thought.

Every ten minutes or so I'd check through the laundry window to see if she was behaving herself. After all, I'd only just recently planted cauliflower and cabbage seedlings. Sure enough, half the seedlings were ripped out and scattered all over the veggie patch. But the pup? What was up with her? She was dragging her behind across the lawn like a single furrow plough in ever increasing circles, every now and then she'd stop and try and bite her tail.

I looked, then with a second take, I saw the offending irritant hanging from her behind. "What the?"

Making my way down to the backyard I called her to me, but she wasn't having any of that. I finally caught up with her on one of her sweeps. "What's the matter sweetie?" I asked, interrupting her progress with a quick grab. "What have you done this time?"

I inspected her rear end to discover hanging there, the remains of a stocking I'd used to tie up last year's beans. Could it have gone through her system that quick, or was it the result of yesterday's expedition? It didn't matter, I had to try and get it out and relieve her anxiety, and mine.

I put her down and grabbed the stocking, for a few moments she remained stationary then with a yelp took off like a Bondi tram. The stocking, reaching the limits of its elasticity, stretched to breaking point, then with a slushy sigh gave way, recoiling straight back into my face, with Rani doing a neat tumble turn on the lawn. I couldn't get to the garden hose quick enough, what with gagging and retching, and my lunchtime lamb casserole just didn't taste the same anymore. Yeah, I know, real funny.

Over the coming years she developed into a wonderful canine companion. She'd learnt all the sit, stay, come, fetch commands and even improvised a few of her own. While we were eating meals she figured out that if she picked up her bowl and presented herself sitting in our presence, she might get some leftovers. What a sight, to see her sitting there quietly with her bowl, a large shiny chrome-plated dish hanging from her mouth. How could we not comply?

Always, when leaving the house, fetching my hat became a daily ritual. I'd place, or even hide it somewhere in the house and ask "where's my hat?" This was the trigger for a hide-and-seek game where she'd search for the golden chalice.

Every room, every corner, under cushions, in cupboards, until eventually she'd march in proudly with gleaming eyes and wagging stump with the prize firmly grasped between her teeth to proclaim her success. She also knew the reward was a run outside with me.

People have asked about the stump. Her tail was lopped as a pup prior to us getting her, but despite some schools of thought, I personally didn't mind it. I like the look, and being a house dog, if

the tail wasn't lopped, there would have been nothing left on the coffee table, she was such a happy dog.

She was also a hunting dog and became a great retriever, quail and duck being her specialty, although there were a few hiccups.

On one occasion while hunting along the Loddon River near Dingwall, I happened upon a lone teal which I dropped with my old double-barrelled shotgun. It landed halfway up the bank on the other side of the river.

I commanded, "fetch", and off she set. Running down the bank she stopped to peer inquisitively over her shoulder obviously wanting to know where the bridge was. "I'm not going in that cold water." "Go on fetch," I repeated, this time with meaning on my voice. She again baulked, walking up and down the bank, not sure what to do. I picked up a three-foot dry branch and hurled it across the narrow river in the direction of the duck. It hit the dry bank did a neat pirouette in the air and landed gently beside the duck, so close the narrow end was touching. "Fetch," I repeated. "Ah, that's what you want," her thought processes kicked in. With an energetic leap she catapulted herself at full stretch into the murky water, swam the river, located the stick and, completely ignoring the duck, retrieved the stick to my feet, pleased as punch and wagging that stump like crazy. "Here's your stick master," she seemed to say.

I couldn't help but admire her energy and ability to follow commands ... to the letter.

Jumping from the bow of the boat when fishing became a little disconcerting, especially when we were underway. She loved the wind in her face, and her floppy ears trailed behind like a couple of airport wind socks, she enjoyed the water immensely. I finally

got her out of that habit but I had to stay alert and be ready to cut the motor, just in case.

She's gone to God now after fifteen and a half years of loyal, devoted companionship and resides in a grave overlooking the house dam she used to love to swim in.

I've heard that Heaven is reserved for humans only. If that is the case, the alternative (whatever that is) might be preferred by those pet owners who wish to be reunited. But, as the answer requires one to be dead, I'm not in a hurry to find out.

Big Colin

During the early sixties, as a young trade's apprentice, I was employed by the Commonwealth Department of Housing and Construction, based at Glen Iris, a south-eastern Melbourne suburb. From that base, crews of tradesmen from all trades were contracted to carry out repairs, alterations and maintenance on a multitude of commonwealth government sites. The variety of establishments was wide, ranging from post offices, munitions factories, army barracks, HMAS Cerberus, Government Aircraft Factory, taxation departments, CSIRO, high rise Melbourne skyscrapers, even the gunnery range on the Mornington Peninsula.

Eighty, maybe even ninety, percent of these tradesmen were made up of returned servicemen, including returned prisoners of war. The balance were apprentices like myself and the odd lucky civilian. Lucky, because they got to work with these fantastic men. Decent, honest men who had recently witnessed the hell of war, had seen and experienced the worst that man can inflict on his fellow man, and they still laughed and joked at the end of it.

Men like Wally Roy, a baby-faced, curly-haired, happy-go-lucky bloke, who always had a kind word and friendly advice. He spent years in Changi and saw hundreds of his comrades die on the railroad. Adam Heusden, an ex-merchant marine sailor, whose face was permanently disfigured by brutal Japanese guards smashing him with rifle butts. And dear old Colin (Harry) Greenough, captured and interned twice after escaping an Italian prison camp only to be recaptured by the Germans, then escaped for good.

He told of actually meeting the great German General Rommel, who shook the Australian prisoner's hand. All the Aussies agreed he was a great soldier and a good bloke. Rommel had mutual respect for the Diggers or Desert Rats and once said that he could capture the world with Aussie and New Zealand soldiers.

Colin reminisced about being put to work with civilians in German factories, and Diggers paying chocolates and cigarettes to civilian women for sexual favours in quiet corners of the factories.

During his internment in an Italian prison camp he related how the totally bored guards had given him a week in the hot box (a punishment hole, dug in the open yard, enclosed with corrugated iron walls and roof) for cruelty to dumb animals. He went on, "I was bored shitless, as was every prisoner in camp, and to amuse myself I was lying on the ground beside an ant nest. As they were coming and going out of the entrance I was donging them on the head. "The bastards gave me a week for that."

On another occasion, an Italian guard was leaning against the barbed wire gate with his hands crossed above the muzzle of his rifle. It discharged, the bullet went through both hands. Internees cheered and mocked at his misfortune.

After escaping and being recaptured, he was sent to a German POW camp where he was forced to work in a coal mine with fellow prisoners overseen by German civilians.

The Australians did not take kindly to being forced to do what civilians told them and deliberately went out of their way to make life difficult. Colin remembered, "There was this officious little prick who delighted in ordering the prisoners of war around. A sadistic little bastard. We were down a dark drive in the mine, even with the carbide light supplied on our helmets you could hardly see a thing. I was squatting against the coalface with a book, pretending to read it. I didn't even know if it was the right way up, but I knew it was really pissing this bloke off. He ran at me screaming gibberish, and laid into me with a bloody shovel, I'd had enough. I stood and dropped him cold with my helmet.

"Next thing the real German guards and an officer were marching me to the surface where they stood me up against a brick wall. The Officer in charge ordered the guards to, ready aim. Then, with a smile, to lower arms. I shit myself. He told me I was on my last chance, so I was a good boy for a while."

After being moved to a glass factory Colin and a mate escaped in a sand truck and were secreted away for the remainder of the war by a friendly Polish family.

Having experienced that lot, Colin had no fear of any man or situation. Employed by the Commonwealth Government after the war, a form was sent to all employees to fill out. On reaching the "dependants" question, he wrote, "all you bastards in 339 Bourke Street." He was summoned to the head office and ushered into the elaborate office of the top director for a "please explain".

"What's the meaning of this," the boss said, flinging the form across the desk in animated disgust, leaning forward with both fists clenched on the desk.

"Listen mate," said Colin, raising himself to his full six-feet-two-inch height. "I've had Rommel trying to intimidate me, what

chance do you really think you've got? As far as the form goes, it's a known fact that one of us workers keeps ten of you bastards in a job." Colin was a big man with a slow, considered drawl, and quite up for the job of returning any intimidation. The director, taken aback, recoiled and stammered back, "Well, d-d-don't d-d-do it again, okay? Now, would you care for a cuppa tea?" "Love one," said Col, and for his reprimand he was served tea and biscuits by the man in charge.

Jonesy

Then there was Jonesy, probably the filthiest man I've ever met. He was employed as a tradesman painter for the Department of Housing and Construction. He was an obese, slovenly man, slow to move, lazy and absolutely disgusting. His face never grew hair and his facial skin hung on his cheeks like old turkey wattles. His entire body wobbled like a jelly when he walked. He suffered from some sort of disability that gave him the permanent shakes. One never followed him after a visit to the toilet, as not only was it more than likely there would be faeces on the door handle, he never washed his hands. His farts were the most disgusting sounds a human could make. For some reason one could hear them coming long before they actually came and when they did exit, they resembled hot, wet laval gases bubbling to the surface.

To actually sit with him at the lunch table was a marathon of tolerance. He loved grapes, but because of his disability, was not able to carefully pluck a single grape from the stem, his hand would shake and slide down the entire length of the stem, showering the table and anybody unlucky enough to be within range. One evening, after a day's work, the leading hand was changing from his work boots into his travelling shoes to discover half a dozen squashed grapes in the base of his shoe; but only after putting it on.

An incident that had grown men gagging occurred when Jonesy asked me to purchase two pieces of couta down at the fish shop on my lunch order trip. (Couta, was a popular fish purchase in those days.) Everyone had washed up for lunch, carpenters, plumbers and painters, and had settled down around the lunch table for a quiet meal.

Jonesy opened up his lunch order, wrapped a piece of greasy couta in paper and proceeded to scoff it down. He was no dainty eater. Eyes began to dart around the table and newspapers raised a little to hide the sight. But there was no escaping the sucks and slops and slurps as he proceeded to devour his meal. But that was nothing compared to what was to come.

Jonesy started to hawk, a Couta bone had lodged in his throat ... he gagged and hawked and coughed and retched, making all in the room stop their dining to watch in amazement the chain of events unfolding before them. After nearly turning blue, and what seemed like an eternity, he hawked up a huge pile of partially eaten Couta onto his fish wrapping. Everybody had stopped eating, some had already got to their feet to leave the room. The final straw came, when everybody, to a man, had to leave the room for the clean fresh air of the outside garden. He then combed through the pile of white mush in search of the offending bone, which, once discovered was placed to one side, while he shovelled the entire slop back into his mouth. Even hardened returned soldiers were feeling crook.

The Pussycat Incident

Jock was a painter with the Department of Housing and Construction. Crews from the Glen Iris depot were sent to all government installations as far away as HMAS Cerberus at Crib Point, post offices all over the suburban sprawl of Melbourne, Army, Navy and Air Force establishments and a myriad of Commonwealth Government sites around the state.

One such venue that required Jock's skills was the Government Aircraft Factory at Fisherman's Bend. This was a huge complex on the banks of the Yarra River near the ports of the City of Melbourne. It saw the construction of such things as the pilotless Jindivic aircraft, the Wirraway, Boomerang, and a number of experimental aircraft of Australian design.

Every morning, thousands of government employees made their way down the cobblestone surface of Lorimer Street, where, at the rear of the bouncing bus, red-blooded young apprentices, surrounded by beautiful belles from the typist pools, were to experience unwanted and embarrassing arousals brought on by the vibrating cobblestones on their new-found, maturing libido, there, to exit the said vehicle at the terminus, not only last but slightly stooped ... but I digress.

On arrival, guards checked all personnel passes for permission to enter the site. One might have mistakenly guessed that Jock was one of the office personnel by his un-tradesman-like attire – suit coat, collar and tie and pork pie hat, all topped off with an imitation crocodile skin Gladstone bag. Doctors of the day dressed less well than Jock.

After donning his hat to a dozen pretty ladies, he picked his way through the complex, which consisted of huge workshops, administration buildings, and paved streets to the rear south-eastern rim of the site to where the small portable change room-cum-workshop and tearoom was located beside the test airstrip. Here he fastidiously removed his clothing, neatly folding the shirt, coat and tie, placing his hat on top and sliding the lot into the top shelf of his locker. Then, dressed with bib and brace overalls and work boots, his morning ritual was complete, he was ready for work.

There were as many as a dozen men in the shed and all were allocated tasks and directions by the leading hand. All except Jock. For jock was his own man, a specialist, a French polisher, his orders came from the top. French polishing was done in many varied and wondrous locations, including the main administration block, or Bullshit Castle, as the returned vets called it, wherever oak-stained doors or wood-grained finishes on office partitions, conference tables, cabinets and assorted furnishings required maintenance. Jock's considerable skills fitted the task admirably.

He was also one for practical jokes. After being admonished by one of the head honchos for helping himself to the man's personal stock of export coffee, he conspired to extract revenge.

All tradesmen started at either 7:30 or eight a.m. Top brass at nine a.m. This gave Jock a small window of time to admit himself to Bullshit Castle while the cleaners were performing their morning's duties. He worked quietly and unseen.

There, outside the boss's office, he deposited, on a length of toilet paper, an expertly fashioned and shaped, plaster turd, stained in brown umber and tipped off with red, beside which he poured a neat pool of shellac.

The resulting tirade was music to Jock's ears, but the poor old cleaners copped the brunt of it all and were ordered to clean up the unsightly mess.

But the most memorable exploit that elevated Jock to hero status became known as "The Pussycat Incident".

At the end of a day's work or shift, those wishing to leave the complex would have to queue at the exit gates where guards checked all bags prior to giving permission to vacate the premises. Jock had noticed at the rear of the site a cat that had recently given birth to a litter of lively kittens. Despite being reasonably young they were still a handful and virtually wild. With the aid of a hessian bag, Jock managed to secure one without being bitten and, placing it gingerly in his Gladstone bag, he clipped the fasteners shut. As the four p.m. shift ended the siren sounded and a human tsunami streamed towards the exit gates. Jock manoeuvred himself into the front of the queue, ensuring any holdups would unsettle those behind, and approached the exit gate.

Most personnel were on first name terms with the guards and as he arrived at the barrier he was greeted with "Okay, Jock me boy, what have you got to declare?" "G'day Bill," said Jock. "Look mate, I've just spent an hour trying to catch one of those wild kittens for my grand-kids, I'd rather you not open the bag."

"Yeah, right, I bet you wouldn't," declared Bill. "Come off it, mate, open the bloody bag." "You open it, and be it on your head if it escapes." The guard, peered over Jock's shoulder at the ever increasing queue, then grasped the bag and flung open both sides. With a squeal, the kitten launched itself into the air and attached a hooked claw into Bill's right ear before disappearing through the amused spectators' legs and out of sight.

"You bloody pest, now look what you've done," bellowed Jock. "Now I have to go and catch him all over again."

"Sorry Jock," Bill replied repentantly. "I just didn't think ..."

"No you bloody well didn't!" cut in Jock. "I'll be back."

With that, Jock returned to the empty workshop where he made a hot cup of tea and settled back to read the sport section of *The Herald* to while the time away. A good half hour elapsed and finally Jock slipped the door ajar and, as the coast was clear, sauntered around the back of the shed to where, among the rubbish and empty paint tins, he'd stashed a beautiful little electric motor – the reason for this whole charade.

He was a keen exotic fish enthusiast and the plan was for this little electric motor to be rigged up as a tank aerator ... if the plan worked. Securing it in the Gladstone bag, he again approached the exit gates. Bill, with a new band-aid applied on his right ear, nodded knowingly and waved Jock through wishing, "all the best" to Jock's grand-kids, and "next please". The Pussycat Incident was achieved.

Jock was also a bit of an alcoholic. Unlike the rest of the crew, he preferred a beer at morning tea and lunch breaks. Drinking on the job was forbidden and he was on his last warning from the foreman, Dick. The men had all settled down to morning tea when Dick rolled up in the Bedford truck. He was a big man and

loomed into the hut like John Wayne through the batwing doors of a Mexican bar. He acknowledged all the men, exchanging pleasantries and nodded approvingly at Jock.

"Well done Jock, keep up the good work, that's what I like to see," he praised Jock warmly. Jock raised the tin of tomato juice in good health, and took a large swig. "Nectar of the Gods", he replied. Business done, materials delivered, Dick said his goodbyes and took off back to Glen Iris. "Okay boys, back to work," the leading hand ordered. As they all stood to resume their tasks, Jock threw the empty tomato juice can into the waste bin revealing a tomato juice label detach itself from a Vic Bitter beer can. He'd done it again.

The Warren

One of the Government buildings that we had the pleasure of working on was Anzac Hostel in North Road, Brighton. A huge, fabulous mansion purchased by the Repatriation Department in 1918. It was officially opened to returned veterans in July 1919.

Originally known as Kamesburgh, this wonderful mansion boasted forty rooms, including nineteen bedrooms, beautifully painted floral ceilings, a wonderful grand staircase, drawing, sitting and dining rooms and a library. Externally, the fantastic gardens included curved paths that led past sunken gardens, standard rose displays, mass plantings of pansies and a dozen other beautiful floral displays, with seating under huge, spreading oak trees, tall exotic palms accented the entrance drives, all attended to by a team of expert gardeners and groundsmen.

At the rear were stone constructed stables, pigeon lofts and a variety of other buildings. I recall that a copper weathercock, in the shape of a fox, adorned the slate roof of the stables and sported a musket ball hole that was reportedly fired from the balcony of the main mansion some eighty yards away. It was here that I, as an apprentice, was permitted my first experience of climbing and working from a forty-foot ladder. It was a huge, heavy Oregon pine construction that required four men to raise into position. Two to foot the base while the other two walked under the frame lifting as they walked towards the footers. Once up, the operator climbed the ladder, usually with one hand as the other held the required tools for the job at hand.

I quite enjoyed working from this height, once up there, but getting there could be hairy. As one scaled each step the heavy flexible frame would belly towards the wall up to two feet and return with a slow even rhythm. One had to hold on tight and time each step with the flexing. The base had to be tied and footed by two men and if possible the top tied as well, as it was apt to slide in windy conditions or on mossy, slippery surfaces. All adding to my learning experience.

The head gardener's name was Bert, a nice fellow, always up for a yarn or joke and very knowledgeable in the art of horticulture. He was complaining bitterly one day about the resident rabbit population which was decimating his seedling plantings. "Have you ever tried to trap them?" I enquired, knowing shooting was out of the question. "Of course," he replied, "they won't go near the damn things." Fancying myself as a bit of a hunter-gatherer I returned, "Do you mind if I have a go?"

"Knock yourself out, mate. I'll show you where there's a burrow." He led me to the east side of a large recreation building and pointed out the entrance under the baseboards.

Next evening, before finishing work, I laid a trap on the run from the burrow, being careful to protect the trip with paper, and smoothing the disturbed run with a soft tea-tree branch. I finished it all off with a handful of crushed rabbit droppings over the entire trap and run.

Bert was beaming as I arrived at work the next morning. "You beauty, you've got one," he exclaimed happily. Sure enough, there in the trap was an exceptionally large buck which Bert had dispatched earlier. I couldn't believe my good fortune, trapping rabbits in the suburbs of Melbourne. This was great.

At morning tea, all the tradies made their way to the tearoom supplied by the hostel. A dank, dark, musty room down a flight of narrow stone steps under the south side of the mansion. Bert was there extolling the virtues of my trapping abilities to all and sundry. I was well pleased with my efforts. "Where can I set my trap this time?" I enquired of him. "Well," he considered thoughtfully, "there is another warren down near the stables." "Near the stables, I haven't seen anything down there." "Well, there is mate, you go check it out". So off I set down the gravel path that led towards the stables. Every so often, I'd stop and look back to discover Bert and most of the crew following my progress intently. George waved me further down the path, "a bit more, mate."

I arrived opposite the stables and turned 360 degrees in vain searching for some sign of ground disturbance, to no avail. He waved to the left. "In there, mate." On the left side there was a small brick building with no windows and a set of solid doors. I pointed, "Yes mate," he yelled, "in there."

I thought, "They must have dug under the building and have an entrance inside." So I gently lifted the latch and entered the building. It was as dark as pitch, but I found a light switch on the architrave. I switched it on. There in front of me was a solid brick table with a black, flecked marble top, and on the table was a stone cold body. Yes a dead body. It was the morgue.

I could hear the laughter coming from up the path, and when I exited with enquiring outstretched arms, it was all made clear to me.

"What's this all about?" I asked, not understanding. Bert, with tears in his eyes replied, "You wanted a warren, you got one. George Warren's his name, he died last night, mate."

It was explained to me that Mr Warren, a Gallipoli veteran had passed during the night. He was one of the last men to have a wheelie bed. Apparently he wouldn't let the nurses take it from him until he died.

I'd copped a bit over the years as an apprentice, being sent down the street for muff buns, left handed hammers, and striped paint, but this one topped the chart.

[Footnote: A Google earth search of the mansion shows that all the beautiful gardens and grounds on the east side are now a jungle of buildings, making up what is now the new Anzac Hostel, with the mansion turned into a school. But surprise, a streetscape view of the southern entrance in Downes Avenue, still shows the stables, the white building on the left and the fox weathercock on the roof, but more, the little brick building on the right, just inside the gate, which was the morgue ... It's still there.]

Acknowledgments

Thanks to my wife Faye for her continued support, encouragement and assistance in producing this work. Also to those dear friends, workmates and returned servicemen that confided in me with their personal tales.

Thanks to Ewen Withers, a magician with computers for his expertise in helping to prepare the final draft of this work and retrieving lost info and images.

Thanks also to Maureen Davenport for her advice and assistance and to Bernie Schultz for the book layout and proofreading.

www.ingramcontent.com/pod-product-compliance
Lightning Source LLC
Chambersburg PA
CBHW031420290426
44110CB00011B/461